KU-224-206

Contents

Contents

SURVIVING OFFICE POLITICS

COPING AND SUCCEEDING IN
THE WORKPLACE JUNGLE

Patrick Forsyth

Marshall Cavendish

Copyright © 2011 Patrick Forsyth
Cover design: Jim Banting

Published in 2011 by Marshall Cavendish Business
An imprint of Marshall Cavendish International

PO Box 65829, London EC1P 1NY, United Kingdom.
info@marshallcavendish.co.uk

and

1 New Industrial Road, Singapore 536196
genrefsales@sg.marshallcavendish.com
www.marshallcavendish.com/genref

Other Marshall Cavendish offices: Marshall Cavendish Corporation. 99 White Plains
Road, Tarrytown NY 10591-9001, USA • Marshall Cavendish International (Thailand)
Co Ltd. 253 Asoke, 12th Flr, Sukhumvit 21 Road, Klongtoey Nua, Wattana, Bangkok
10110, Thailand • Marshall Cavendish (Malaysia) Sdn Bhd. Times Subang, Lot 46,
Subang Hi-Tech Industrial Park, Batu Tiga, 40000 Shah Alam, Selangor Darul Ehsan,
Malaysia

Marshall Cavendish is a trademark of Times Publishing Limited

A CIP record for this book is available from the British Library

ISBN 978-981-4351-06-5

Printed in Singapore by Fabulous Printers Pte Ltd

Marshall Cavendish publishes an exciting range of books
on business, management and self-development.

If you would like to:

- Find out more about our titles
- Take advantage of our special offers
- Sign up to our e-newsletter

Please visit our
special website at: www.business-bookshop.co.uk

Foreword

Probably the most useful book you will ever buy

If you want to help improve the efficiency or profitability of the organisation in which you work, learn about the latest management technique, or improve a basic skill— like making a presentation or thinking laterally—then this book is not going to help you one tiny bit. If, on the other hand, you want to excel, progress or even just survive in the jungle of the modern office, then this is very much the book for you. Get a copy quickly, before any of your colleagues do so, or they will very quickly cease to be colleagues and become rivals —adversaries even—if they are not such already.

This book can make the difference between success and failure, between top management and office junior, between a life of jet-setting and excitement and total boredom in a job where the most challenging task is polishing the transparencies in window envelopes, for instance.

So buy it now. Doing so may be the first act by the new YOU. The YOU who is not going to be put upon any more, who is going to be a force to be reckoned with, who is going to play a key role and have everyone appreciate it. Of course, you may be a survivor already; or even be on top of it all now—Megalomania Inc. personified. If you are, you will not need persuading to buy this book. You will realise all too well that this state of affairs does not just happen; it is not a matter of chance. You will have been working at it, and know that if this book gives you even a smidgen more ammunition that might be just what is needed to keep you safely ahead of the game in the future, it will be worth every cent.

Whichever category you are in, buying this book could be the best investment that you would ever make during your career. It is, in all conscience, a modest enough investment considering what is at stake. So buy it for goodness sake, you are never going to have time to take it all in just browsing in the shop before a member of staff comes round and throws you out for loitering. Besides, lengthy browsing will make people think it is salacious, which it is not (if you want one of those books, they are the ones that are cellophane wrapped—to keep the dirt in), and you may ruin the author's fragile literary reputation.

Once you have it, read it and then, go straight back to the office. Next time someone suggests you are all burnt out, instead of confessing that you never really caught fire, you will be able to show him or her that assuming you have had a charisma by-pass operation is a big—no, huge—mistake.

❝In my company we are so confused, we are stabbing each other in the chest.**❞**

(Overheard in conversation amongst
delegates at a management course)

Sex

Now there is a good heading to get in early on in the piece. Why? Well, writing this book was proceeded by considerable research. All the best books are preceded by considerable research, in this case not least amongst those with whom I liaise at the publisher's. These include the Editor, the Assistant Editor, the publishing assistant, several secretaries, the receptionist and the person who delivers the tea (thank you—milk, no sugar for me). They are all, to my certain knowledge, women. This, together with other observations over the years, confirms that there are, in fact, many women working in all sorts of capacities in organisations of every type. And most of them are very capable too.

The English language, however, has yet to come up with a single word that means 'he or she', and while some terminologies—such as chairperson—have come into common usage, other phrases, however innocently intended, can appear inappropriately sexist. I would like to make it clear at this stage, prompted only by about six editorial staff with total power over my royalties, that there is no intention hereafter to imply anything other than that women are equal partners with men in the workplace.

Women may be in the minority amongst those who

work in offices but often, they are amongst the most professional—and well aware of both of these facts.

66 Men play the game; women know the score. 99

Roger Woddis

66 Women would rather be right than reasonable. 99

Ogden Nash

Key guidelines to success

Always remember:

- Getting to the top is like trying to climb a pyramid, there is more room for people at the slopes than at the top. Remember too that the upper slopes can hold comparatively fewer people; the minions on the lower slopes, at least, have numbers on their side —some people must surely succeed.

- Position without power is very common. In other words, even amongst the people near the top, there are many who are going no further and whose positions are more precarious than they may appear at first sight. You may find the thought of being near the top, but toothless, less than appealing.

- Success, or lack of it, is not preordained. There are secrets to be learnt and success, at least in part, goes to those who use them to work the system.

So within the following pages, the stage and the activities that take place on it are turned upside down and shaken to see what goes on, and where—amongst the absurdities of office life—the opportunities may be found. There are real principles involved here that can help smooth your path to success. Read, mark, learn and inwardly digest: there may be some amongst them that can give you just the 'edge' you need.

As a start:
- Do not be led by events—take the initiative, work at your priorities.
- Sex may sometimes look like a short cut to success; more likely it is a direct route to trouble. It is, after all, rather difficult to say "You're fired" when both parties are in bed, certainly if it is the same bed. Booze is a similar hazard. Sometimes a political move that feels as if it will be best preceded by a large gin and tonic, is better executed with a clear head. In most organisations people would rather promote the office cat than anyone with even a hint of a drinking problem. In any case, success may be important, but is it sufficiently important to lay down your liver for?

So:
- Always stay more sober than your opponent.

Office Politics in Context

All, nothing or something

Unless your office is the exception (though if it is why are you reading this?), it may be that you have noticed that in others, whilst on the surface they run smoothly, efficiently and with hardly a murmur to interrupt the air of pleasant calm, there can be something of an underlying hint of intrigue. In others, again, there is an unconcealed hotbed of rivalry, enmity and backbiting. If you were to find yourself in such an environment you would doubtlessly stand back from it, stay neutral and uninvolved, and get on with the job. And if you find a single person who believes that, then take immediate steps to sell him Tower Bridge.

Even if you did stand back from it all, would you thrive? The trouble with being in the middle of the road is the pronounced tendency to get run over. And the less said—about what sitting on the fence does to you—the better.

In most organisations some degree of office politics is one of the 'givens'. Indeed, it is normal and perhaps, given human nature, inevitable. But what does this mean exactly?

On the one hand it conjures up a picture of jockeying for a place on the Board, fighting to become Head of Department, or plotting to take over as Managing Director or Chief Executive. On the other hand, office politics includes a level of activity at which the goal is seeing who can get the most praise, the biggest salary increase, the best office, the prettiest secretary, the most up to date mobile phone or just the seat nearest the window. What is more, and make no mistake about this, the most vicious infighting is often over the comparatively small prizes. Hell hath no fury like that of those who feel that they have been unjustly denied the key to the Executive Washroom. This is, after all, not something you can forget and indeed, you will doubtlessly be reminded of it several times a day as you go about your ablutions.

These undercurrents show themselves in a hundred and one different ways each day. They show in conversation—in the insults —"There are only two things I don't like about you—your face"; in the rumours—"I hear that what's his name in Research is up for the chop"; in a dozen different phrases that are designed not to help but to stir things up in some way. They show in the manoeuvring for position, in the bluff and double bluff, in the way that even the mildest mannered employees can be roused to fury by the feeling that they have been slighted, and in the way in which even the most well positioned individuals still seem to strive for more. Everyone seems to be after something, whether it is control of the whole organisation or just a new filing cabinet (after all, even the person who already has everything would still want a nice 'something' or 'somewhere' to keep his or her things in). And whether you get what you want or not, be your ambition large or small, it does matter—at least it does to you.

So realistically, whether we admit it or not, office politics is something that involves everybody to some degree. The question is, therefore, what do you do about it? How involved do you get and what do you have to watch for, watch out for and do? There is, of course, no single nice neat answer. There is no one thing you can do that will whisk you to the top of the organisational hierarchy; certainly no magical gesture like snapping your fingers and shouting, "Promotion!" Like so much in organisational life, achieving success is bereft of magic formulae. There are, however, a variety of aspects of office life through which you can exert some positive influence or use to watch your back.

Hence this book: it reviews those aspects in turn so as to cast some light on how they may help or hinder your progress. It may be presented in a light-hearted manner but it aims to impart some good sense along the way. Winning the workplace battle is not, to say the least, an exact science. Without care, planning and guile you are left subject to circumstances and other peoples' ambition. You are apt to end up like a midget dancing with a lady of abundant bust—unable either to see where you are going or even to hear the music.

Overall, there are only two ways of setting out to win the office war. If you are to progress unscathed through the war zone, if you are not just to survive but to prosper, one approach is to just do a good job, trusting that the powers that be will notice what you do and, that virtue will bring its own reward. You may believe this is sufficient. You may be right. Good work and a measure of good luck may be enough. There is evidence aplenty, however, that doing a good job does not automatically always get the recognition it deserves and certainly, looking like a doormat almost guarantees to get you trodden on. As for good luck, that can only ever be certainly relied upon to explain the success of your rivals.

Alternatively, you can do both a good job and work at ensuring that people—the right people—*do* notice so that you would get the recognition you deserve and achieve some of your other goals along the way. The latter approach may be a safer bet, and working on being successful is even more important if you are not in fact doing a good job—which is exactly what some of those who thrive in business do.

66 Everybody was up to something, especially, of course, those who were up to nothing. 99
Noel Coward

The trouble with the office war is that not everything is what it seems. Before proceeding any further, let us look at the very first point at which the truth of this becomes clear: before you even get into an office. It may be a good moment, if it is not already too late, to consider whether you really want to work in an office amongst the unfettered cut and thrust at all, particularly one concerned with the sordid world of business and commerce (though any organisation, profit making or not, has its less attractive aspects). You could opt instead to do something away from the seemingly inevitable friction that appears to surround groups of people. You could become a solitary lighthouse keeper, a perpetual solo round-the-world sailor, or just a hermit. But the options for complete avoidance seem rather limited. Even that new breed—the home-workers—have to meet other people some of the time. But we digress; even before you get into the office world everything is not necessarily what it seems. Somebody says to you, "You may be interested in this opportunity ..." It may be that a job advertisement is pointed out to you, it might be that a headhunter telephones you, or just that a colleague at work offers you a useful snippet of news. But is it an opportunity?—*An opportunity to get in on the ground floor.* Sounds good, but it may well mean the company or department referred to is small, insignificant or underfinanced—or all three. Hearing someone say, "You will be part of a new management structure," should prompt you to wonder or ask what became of the old one. "Full training will be given," might mean they cannot find anyone who knows how to do 'it', or that they will lend you the manual. "Commission guaranteed for six months ..." and then what? As you investigate further, other facts or phrases should act as warning signs. A lack of job description may mean wonderful flexibility or that no one has thought about what it should say. An expense account may mean unlimited spending or a major battle every time you charge for a taxi ride, even if going by bus needs three hours planning and the same amount of time standing at the bus stop while those of the wrong number sail past you in convoy.

Most important of all, why should someone be pointing you towards any sort of opportunity anyway? Out of the goodness of their heart, or because they want you out of the way? Those who intend to survive habitually question everything, especially the motives of other people, even those who offer something attractive—correction, especially those who offer something attractive. A healthy cynicism is a necessary characteristic of all those who intend to win out in the office jungle.

Assuming you are already working in an office, or refuse to be put off doing so, the first thing to take into account is the other people who will be there.

❝ The world is divided into people who do things—and people who get the credit. **❞**
Dwight Morrow

Ten phrases that should sound warning bells
- "I can honestly say ..."
- "I'm from head office and here to help."
- "I'm only saying this for your own good ..."
- "I'm sure no one knows about it."
- "It is perfectly simple."
- "Now, there is nothing personal in this ..."
- "Of course, I'm on your side in this ..."
- "You may not believe this, but ..."

- "I thought of you immediately."
- "Trust me."

Megalomania (un)Limited

Imagine. This is an organisation which, almost certainly, has nothing in common with the one you work for. Most of what goes on there can be categorised as activity rather than achievement. There are more Chiefs than Indians. More time seems to be spent in meetings, on committees and at crisis point than in actually delivering customer satisfaction. For all its high-powered image, its plush offices (imagine Singapore's Orchard Road or the floors above the Emporium in Bangkok) and its market standing, it can be a difficult place to work in. Decision-making tends to be a long and drawn out process, internal procedures are labyrinthine and yet, despite all this—perhaps because of it—everyone is very busy in one way or another ...

Megalomania Case No 1: *You scratch my back...*
George Lane and Mary Lee were Area Managers, reporting to one of the 10 Megalomania Regional Directors. Now, being a Regional Director was a good job. It carried with it a large car, real authority and, with a staff to actually do the work was, as they say, a nice little number. Both George and Mary had their sights set on such a job. What was more, their own Director's assistant (Director's Assistant was a good position in itself and a direct route to being a Director), was due to retire in six months.

Mary played every trick in the book to put herself in line. She stayed close to the Director. Her communications stepped up, her image was polished; even her administration was faultless. More so when she saw George was also spending time with the Director, and with his retiring assistant. *Waste of time, she thought, he won't have any influence on his replacement.*

She was right too. The assistant had no great interest in who replaced him. He did, however, have a pet project and was determined to see that completed to his satisfaction before he left. This he only confided on a limited basis.

In due course, an announcement was made. George was to become Singapore's Regional Manager, a new appointment to co-ordinate all the Area Managers in the Asia/Pacific region. An outsider was being brought in to fill the assistant's role (As the memo said, ... *to move two Area Managers at once would leave our operation vulnerable.*). Mary was not mentioned.

Of course, George was delighted to move from his present base in Europe to the large company house off Singapore's Bukit Timah Road. It would be hot out there, and it would take a while to get used to how everything worked in that part of the world, but the salary, benefits and opportunity made it worthwhile. It has certainly been the right approach with old John to ask what he most wanted to get sorted out before he retired. He would quite enjoy having him to stay occasionally; after all, he knew Asia rather well.

> *Moral:* Set your sights high—and consider and involve the people who help you, do not just use them. You may do better if they do better also.

Ten Potential Allies

Your boss
The accountant
Your secretary
Other people's secretary
The tea lady (who sees and hears everything)
Visiting consultants
Receptionist/Switchboard operator
Central services (e.g. Personnel/Office Management)
The expert (in whatever you are not—computers say)

Ten Potential Enemies

Your boss
The accountant
Your secretary
Other people's secretary
The tea lady (who sees and hears everything)
Visiting consultants
Receptionist/Switchboard operator
Central services (e.g. Personnel/Office Management)
The expert (in whatever you are not—computers say)

Know your enemy

Before we move on, let us pick up a point or two about

one of those listed in the table: the consultant. Consultants have been described as people with their tongue in your ear, their hand in your pocket and their faith in your gullibility. They are accused of borrowing your watch to tell you the time, and then keeping the watch. In fact, consultants can be very valuable (and though you would expect me to say that, I do believe it is true—in most cases). They do all sorts of things—acting as everything from visiting firemen to ad hoc directors and performing all sorts of discreet one-off tasks (like, in my case, training). They may be used for their specialist expertise or their objectivity, or both. And, make no mistake, they are sometimes used to distance management from unpopular decisions: *I know people were made redundant, but the consultants said it was the only way.* Whatever they do, they tend to get to know a good deal about the organisations for which they work. They may also be retained at a senior level and thus have the ear of key players. As such, they can be a useful source of information and make better allies than enemies. Think twice before you kick one out of your office and say, "I'm too busy."

66 In this company it is all management by crony. 99

(Overheard in the corridor)

Now let us turn to the environment in which all this and more takes place.

The political stage

The world of work has never presented people with a greater challenge.

Business pundits and economists predict a range of varying scenarios for the future of the work environment. Incidentally, predicting is easy—it is making sure that your predictions prove correct that is difficult. Putting that aside, however, one thing all such pundits are sure about is—the future will be uncertain. We live in dynamic times. The old world of job security, jobs for life, prescribed ladders of promotion and gradually increasing success and rewards has gone, replaced by talk of re-organisation, downsizing, fixed-term contracts, redundancy, teleworking, and portfolio careers.

Forgive the overlay of gloom and the glut of jargon terms (a glut of jargon is something that characterises the modern organisation). Let us be clear: re-organisation may be for all sorts of good reasons, but it means trouble for some people. Downsizing almost sounds positive, but it means reducing numbers and *getting rid of people* and calling it 'rightsizing' makes it no different. Redundancy also means getting rid of people, though it implies staying on the right side of employment legislation as you do it. Again, be warned. If you are offered teleworking, it means your job is rated so highly that it is regarded as possible for you to do it remotely by telephone—a minimal shed in the wilds of faraway Shetland awaits. Portfolio careers suit some people (I would have mine no other way), but a switch from full-time employment to such an arrangement can still bode ill. Organisations must recognise new realities and adopt new approaches to stay ahead in an increasingly competitive world too. This makes them less sympathetic to the individual. It makes them more likely to operate on a short-term basis and it makes people in them defensive, self-seeking and, at worst, aggressive.

For the individual, waiting for things to 'get back to normal' is simply not one of the options. No one can guarantee a successful career for himself or herself, though it is something that everyone can influence to some degree. Indeed, it is something that you surely want to influence. We all spend a great deal of time at work thus it is important to make this time as enjoyable and rewarding as possible. There is a line in one of John Lennon's songs—*Life is what happens while you are making other plans*—which encapsulates a painful thought. Situations in which you must look back to and then say something to yourself that begins with "If only ..." are perhaps the worst positions to get into.

With a rigid, preordained career ladder for the individual to follow unlikely these days, the prospects of success cannot be assumed. Similarly, with turbulent markets for organisations to operate in, and dynamic times ahead, no organisation can regard success as a given. The bad news is that there is no single magic formula guaranteed to ensure overall success. Two things are clear, however. First, having the right skills and competencies is the foundation to being able to do your job well. Secondly, surviving and thriving in a competitive workplace demands that you work actively at career development— some of that activity is just straightforward common sense (though some are more complex than that: refer to my book *Detox your career*), but without a political dimension to it many people will find that they are operating with one hand tied behind their back.

While dwelling on the workplace, it may just be worth touching on something else. You are, I do not doubt, a fine upstanding citizen and a fine upstanding employee too. But be warned, organisations do not assume this. In many organisations, especially large ones, the reverse is assumed. They expect a bad apple or two and they expect a host of minor breaches of etiquette, rules or even the law. So they check up on you. Smile—you may well be on candid camera every working day. All sorts of checking may go on—there is even software that can monitor your computer keystrokes and record exactly what you are up too (so you may want to delete that History now).

So take care. Even your best political moves can be rendered utterly useless by transgressing in some major way and being recorded doing it. Why have organisations become so belligerent in this kind of way? Well, consider the facts that follow:

- 40% of all casual drug users take drugs at work
- 1 in 3 midweek visitors to theme parks and the like are doing so on a dishonestly taken day off
- 1 in 5 workers has had sex with a co-worker at the workplace
- 70% of Internet hits on porn sites are made during working hours

- More people—significantly more people—are away
  sick on Mondays and Fridays than any other day of
  the week

Even allowing for the fact that the statistics come from
the United States (and are QUOTED in *The Living Dead*,
written by David Bolchover [John Wiley]), would they
be so different elsewhere? This is all a little bit worrying.
Anyway, if you are up to no good and are spotted, do not
be surprised—and do not blame me.

So, the stage is set. For good or ill you must operate
in the corporate environment as it is; you must accept the
new realities and never assume a lack of lurking hazards as
such a situation is vanishingly unlikely. Assume the worst
and if the organisation seems a bit like a kindergarten
sometimes, remember that 'what is in the sand box may
well be quick sand'.

> 66 It's always easy to tell a successful executive.
> He's the one who can shift all the responsibility,
> shift all the blame and appropriate all the
> credit. 99
>
> *Ronald Reagan*

Amongst the players

Having hinted at the plethora of different people around an
organisation, they do in fact fall into four clear political types:

- *The political publicists*—who are concerned, above
  all, with appearances, with the impression they are
  making on others, and the recognition they are

getting because of what they are or appear to be rather than what they achieve. They are concerned with everything that shows: the office, the equipment and general paraphernalia which they surround themselves with. Such people will spend a disproportionate amount of time and effort on matters of apparent insignificance. Of course, such things do matter, or at least some of them do. The prime characteristic of political publicists is that they pursue these ends to the exclusion, even to the detriment of the real tasks they have to perform. For example, the political publicist working in customer service will use customers for his own ends rather than putting them first. A complaint about slow service will be blamed on another department—*What I have to put up with*— rather than be given an efficient response and be used as constructive feedback. An image of being a solitary oasis of efficiency in a desert of unreliability may be portrayed, and certain masochistic pleasure derived from the whole incident.

A typical political publicist would be the Export Manager, jetting around the world and delighting in the choice of airline, the frequent traveller cards he collects, the carefully preserved luggage stickers from exotic places on his designer suitcase and the importance of a particular hotel—the one with that excellent Chinese restaurant and the receptionist who always remembers his name. All this is, of course, rated far above coming home with the order. A successful trip is one of good contacts, nights on the tiles in the exotic local dives and collecting hair-raising travellers' tales.

Meanwhile, back at the office where he appears periodically, demanding piles of typing to be done, things are chaotic to say the least. He never has time to spend planning, managing, discussing or for anything very much that will not promote the image he has chosen for himself. Of course, others around him suffer. They have to pick up the pieces, deal with things while he is away, stay late in the office to make phone calls to Sydney or wherever when it is daylight at the other end. They, if they are loyal, will cover for him too, doing the jobs he does not apparently have time for, keeping him out of trouble and receiving little for their pains except to hear his boss occasionally congratulate him for the things with which, in fact, they are coping. There is no justice. So what else is new?

- *The political mole*—Here, the whole strategy is based on secrecy. The mole is the arch exponent of dodging the system, of hiding the facts, hoarding information for the day when it might just be useful—whilst at the same time making himself appear to be indispensable. He takes the old maxim about information being 'power to extremes'. He spends large amounts of time photocopying, and checking to see what interesting documents might have been inadvertently left in the feeder whilst he does so. He seems to be copied with an extraordinary number of e-mails—*Might be best if I was kept informed.* He has large, incomprehensible filing systems, lists of useful contacts whom he spends long moments pumping for information, and a philosophy of looking for what information and circumstances may do for him in the future, rather than for the immediate relevance to the business of the day. If he has staff reporting to him, they are kept forever in the dark, whereas he will have numbers of co-conspirators—fellow moles—with whom he has confidential meetings behind firmly closed doors. He tends to assume that everyone operates in the same way as he does and therefore, sees plots and counter-plots around every corner. He is, therefore, not a great collaborator. Rather, he tends to distrust everyone and regard them as being after 'his' information. When he does use his store of data, it is on a carefully controlled basis—a little here, a little there—making it very clear as he does so what an important service he is rendering in providing the data.

66 I'm not running for President, but if I did I'd win. 99

Donald Trump

A typical mole might work as head of staff of a department such as Personnel or Training. Such a Training Department Manager will always have a great number of slides hidden away, but not a library of slides that anyone else can access. He will include snippets of information in his courses, stressing his privileged position and dropping in the fact that, *I mustn't say more*. He may not, in fact, know very much more but always, the impression given is quite the reverse.

- *The territorial politician*—who is an aggressive empire builder. He wants to be involved in everything. Everything must be routed through him, authorised by him and generally have his two-pennyworth thrown into it. He must be on every management committee, at every important meeting and associated in person and—just interminably—in name, with everything that goes on. If there is a new committee convened say, to consider whether the organisation or department should restructure, he will be on it. If a new procedure is needed, he will suggest it—and of course, it will involve him or his department in a key role. Even if his involvement cannot manifestly be in a key role, he will be in there somewhere with an eye to what is going on. He wants more of everything: more staff, more office space, more equipment, a bigger budget and more regular coffee deliveries. He wants everything he does to be better, more up to date and more state of the art than anyone else around the organisation. He was the first to have a laptop computer and will doubtlessly be the first to have a videophone. At the same time, he is the first to knock other departments. His joy when something goes wrong in some sections other than his own is ill concealed—*I am so sorry to hear …*—and other people in and outside the organisation are treated as unwitting pawns in his game of self-aggrandizement. A customer with a complaint is not a problem to be resolved but an opportunity to take over whatever area has caused the problem, so that it will not happen again—*Someone must sort it out.*

The typical *territorial politician* may inhabit any department. Sometimes, it is an important one with real power as well as tentacles everywhere. Sometimes, it is a small corner containing delusions of grandeur—and with tentacles everywhere.

These character types are themselves readily recognisable—just look around you. But they are not mutually exclusive. In other words, there are those people who exhibit characteristics of two of the types described, or even some of all three. The net result of all these approaches is not, of course, in the best interests of the organisation. These political types are, in fact, intent on the betterment of themselves, their departments and their reputations and rewards even to the point of allowing the organisation's objectives to be met less well. At worst, they allow actual damage to be done in the process. Things may take longer, things may cost more, others may be inconvenienced. They blithely take the view that anything like this is a worthwhile trade-off as long as their own gains are substantial. Profits may be lost, people thrown out of their jobs, customers alienated, but no matter what, as long as they are made head of department or get a new potted plant in their office, all is well.

There is a fourth category. You will have noticed that none of the three so far described includes you, perhaps because you are not at all political. Really? This is unlikely—everyone is to some degree. Anyway, if you are not, what are you doing reading this book? It would seem a little like reading a book on Japanese tea making ceremony when you only drink coffee.

There is another category, however, and you most likely fit into it—the *productive politician*, who deploys a degree of guile from each of the three philosophies, but do so with the broad issues in mind, to advance himself or herself, yes, because he or she honestly believes that the interests of the organisation and himself or herself coincide (well, most of the time).

66 Better to have your enemies inside the tent pissin' out than outside pissin' in. 99
Lyndon Johnson

A little help from your friends

The preceding categories are set out largely so that you can recognise the opposition. However, there are other character types in any organisation—who are more neutral, who gain their satisfaction in other ways than from the rough and tumble of political intrigue—who can be a great help to you or to your rivals. The politically 'ept' cultivate their help and support. Again, the descriptions that follow are not mutually exclusive. People may fill these roles and be neutral or at the same time, political players themselves. More than one role may be played simultaneously.

The first are the *gatekeepers*. They are those who, however significant or not in their own right, are a channel to others of importance. For example, the Secretary or Assistant who has the ear of the boss and can provide—if she has a mind to access—information, advance warning or insight. Or the receptionist—party to so many comings and goings—who is in a position to overhear so much and perhaps pass on a little. Similarly, there is the Office Manager who crosses so many departmental boundaries and has both a wide remit and an extensive information network.

Sometimes there is a chain of *gatekeepers*. One provides access to another who provides access to another and so on. The Accountant, for instance, might be the only one who can get any co-operation from the Finance Director, who in turn has the ear of the Managing Director (M.D.) himself. Such access points are well worth seeking out, cultivating and maintaining contact with on a regular basis. This may be a case of regular liaison. It may involve an exchange of favours—the 'you scratch my back and I'll scratch yours' route. It may even involve some blatant blackmail— suggesting that *unless you can do this then I will, or will not, do something else*. An exchange of this sort can require strong nerves, particularly if you are claiming more power than you actually have. Join a good poker school and pay attention to the teacher.

The second type of supporting player is the *mother hen*. *Mother hens* are often, but by no means always, women. They are those who adopt the role of a professional agony aunt within the organisation—and provide a shoulder for others to cry on. They genuinely enjoy the role of a helper and, if they are good at it, demonstrate one of the most useful attributes for the politically adept—the ability to listen.

Mother hens amass a veritable mine of information about people, more so if they do not obviously betray confidences, and it will include a good deal about peoples' private as well as business lives. They know who is unhappy, unappreciated, or underrated. They know who is on the way up, the way down or the way out. They know who is at loggerheads or in bed together—literally or metaphorically. They make the most useful allies, and they can also make disproportionately dangerous enemies. Their networks do not follow the regular channels. Their influence is not limited to one department or one level of personnel. Because they get satisfaction from their role, they tend to have a considerable and wide ranging effect around the office, despite not necessarily being in a senior or central position themselves. Make sure you know which people are the *mother hens* and resolve to be on good terms with them all.

Others who are also invaluable to the process of seeking advantage include those who are expert on a particular, and to you—useful, topic whether it is the intricacies of the management accounts, the market situation in China, or how to make your intransient computer toe the line. Often, such people—courted as experts, flattered about their expertise and drawing pleasure from demonstrating it—are ready sources of information. And if you know where to go for them and others do not, you have an edge. It is prudent to guard your sources. A similar category pertains to those who—whilst not themselves having the contact or information—know, as the advertisement has it, 'a man who does'. Then there are those who are simply 'useful eyes and ears', who hear things and are prepared to pass them on, at least to you or to a chosen few.

The entire organisation is in fact likely to be a maze and network of useful contacts but there is a need for you to locate, then court and then maintain them. In addition, at least some of them will need a favour or two in return for anything that they do for you. The trick is to find people who can be disproportionately useful to you, and who rate things that are easy for you to do for them highly.

Passages of power

Even if your offices are not grand enough to have the usual corridors of power, they will have a host of places in which people can actually get up to their political shenanigans. Sometimes, it will occur in the office itself. A great deal of interaction, however, takes place either on the move or in a variety of nooks and crannies. You must, if you are to be a dedicated office politician, never be off duty. Do not, for instance, allow yourself to be off guard when some one buttonholes you in the passage, the elevator or the car park. It is possible the conversation has been precisely initiated there so that there is a chance that you will be off guard. Sometimes, a point is best made where time is limited—catching a word on the stairs before you go into a meeting. Or something comes over differently if the venue is informal—what more so than the loo, the kitchen or beside the coffee machine. Other places, even though they are classic places for the quick word, are essentially public—like the reception area. You may be overheard or you may want a witness or something that will restrict the vehemence of the response you expect.

Another factor of the physical environment to keep in mind is that of territory. We all operate differently on our own ground. It may be more difficult to walk into other people's office and tear them off a strip, or fire them, than to do the same thing having called them into your own office. It is wise therefore to choose your ground for some of the exchanges you want to engage in.

Do not, therefore, rush unthinkingly into a major showdown over a cup of coffee in the staff cafeteria. As your voice is raised, it is likely that a deadly hush will descend on the assembled company as every ear in the room tunes in on the row with the precision of so many radar dishes, and people begin to take sides, draw conclusions or work out what there might be for them in the situation they observe.

Conversely, do not let an issue be raised with you on your own, as it were in a corner, if your plan is to deal with it at an open meeting. It has become a cliché that when someone senior says to someone less so, "Come into my office for a moment," there is an automatic assumption that something is wrong. This has its origins not only in bad management practice, but also in our innate sense of territory.

> 66 There is no secret about success. Did you ever know a successful man that didn't tell you about it? 99
>
> *Kin Hubbard*

Key guidelines to success

- *Make sure you know whom you must influence.* It will not always be the obvious people; it will not be the same people for everything you want to achieve; and it will—certainly in a large organisation—involve new people as staff come and go (perhaps some of the going will be hastened by your successes!).
- *Make sure you know, as much as possible, about those you have to influence.* You can do worse than keep a dossier on them (and consider whether it should be kept in your lockable filing cabinet or in your home safe).
- *Check out whom, amongst those you identify, is really in charge.* You can waste a great deal of time and effort on those who seem to be able to help, but who have little influence; and they, of course, will encourage the attention. Look behind the titles.
- *Resist snap judgements.* Always take your time and thoroughly assess people. A second look may give you a second chance, a hasty look may provide no chance at all.

- *Look after your peers; indeed, be seen to do so.* It will help your case if others, up and down the organisation, know you are well supported or at least well connected.
- *Remember: if you can influence the key people, you can be as influential as the key people.* Now having dwelt to an extent on the players and the theatre of the workplace, we will consider, as it were, the make-up. As we shall see, appearances can be deceptive—and sometimes that is exactly what is required.

02

The Power of Image

> ❝ It is only shallow people who do not judge by appearances. ❞
>
> *Oscar Wilde*

First impressions last

You only get one chance to make a good first impression and, whether you like it or not, every aspect of your appearance says a great deal about you. Absurdly, small things have become typecasting. Men with a row of pens in their top outside jacket pocket are immediately categorised, not just as a little uncaring about their appearance but, as lightweight peasants. Women who wear far too much make-up are seen as either tarty or past their sell-by date.

Once upon a time this typecasting was, at least in terms of overall appearance, less the case because of a greater conformity. In some organisations there was, what was in effect, a uniform. It may not have been a written instruction, but it was understood. And so there were grey suits, white shirts and sober ties everywhere you looked and, in this respect therefore, it was difficult for the people in the organisation to make much of an impression unless, of course, they refused to conform. In which case, they were clearly identifying themselves as trouble-makers.

There would then have been calls for their unsuitable tie, or whatever, to be burnt before they were transferred to some distant backwater of the organisation—there to languish until they changed their outlook (and their clothes). Even then, they would probably never be returned to the fold with it all forgotten. Now, of course, this is rarely the case. The days of being able to recognise 'IBM man' even at 50 paces, have gone. Indeed, informality around the office seems to increase day by day. Sometimes, when I conduct a course, say in Singapore, I am the only man wearing a tie. There are still some general rules about personal appearance, however, and certainly there are things that, whilst neither right nor wrong, will tend to be read in a particular way.

Both overall impression and detail are important. We will consider examples of each in turn. First, we focus on the overall impression we give to others.

66An ounce of image is worth a pound of performance. **99**

Anonymous

Overall impression certainly matters, and it does so disproportionately. Consider how even the first glance influences people. It can prompt the policeman to say, "Excuse me, Sir" or "Oi, you." It can prompt someone to say, "What a sight!" or "What are you doing tonight?" It can get you seen as a power to be reckoned with or a damp squid. What is more, all this, or a major part of it, happens with a glance, in just a few seconds. Of course, this is not right: no one can sum people up that quickly—not reliably and accurately anyway. But people try. And impressions they form in this way take some shifting. The moral for the would-be office winner is to look the part. But what does this mean? Doing so is not an exact science of course; there are, however, some common sense rules. Generally speaking, those who rise to the top in organisations look the part. Success, in most peoples' mind, is associated with smartness. Captains of industry do not wear a uniform but they do not look, for the most part, like scarecrows. Some people succeed without conforming. Some do so without even being smart. But if you work in a competitive environment, patronising astronomer Patrick Moore's tailor is probably not to be recommended. Richard Branson, head of the Virgin Group, is renowned for wearing sweaters rather than suits or jackets and ties—but they are very smart sweaters.

Some things about dress and personal appearance, and behaviour are drummed into us at our mother's knee. Do not eat your peas off your knife (at least not unless you put honey on it first to stop the peas from rolling off in all directions) for instance. This does not mean such rules are straightforward to keep. There are often other difficulties. For example:

- *Clean shoes*
  These are certainly a sign of a well turned out and competent person. Easy? Shoes shining when you leave home in the morning, you struggle down the muddy path to the garage and get out the car. You park

your car in a muddy station car park, stand on the platform in the rain, get on the train with other people trampling all over you, and similar traumas await you if you travel by bus. Not surprisingly, you arrive at the office looking as if you wear the cast-off footwear of a manual labourer. Moral: a tin of shoe polish in your desk drawer does wonders for your image, or at least for your feet.

- *A well-pressed suit*
  Similarly important. For a man, it does not need to be grey but should not probably be in a bold mauve checked pattern. Nor should it be too unconventional: corduroy is okay only if the office is associated with something artistic or creative. There are those who will advise, for a fee, on the image that is given by your clothes and personal appearance. For a large fee they will suggest that you do not wear a double breasted suit if you are overweight, as it exaggerates any middle age spread; that you do not wear a white shirt as it will highlight any shaver's rash, or any sign of your having had a touch too much to drink. For an even larger fee, they will pander to your ego and tell you that everything you wear is just right. The fact that such consultants spend a fortune on their own clothes tends to be reflected in their fees.

- *A suitable tie*
  If it is a club tie try to remember which one it is and

do not wear something representative of a fringe cult when lunching with a conservative client. Your tie should not look as if your most tasteless nephew bought it for you; still less as if he did so at the nearest Oxfam charity shop. If your tie has an expensive, exclusive label, wear it only when you want to look that well-off (not to job interviews at which the interviewer is wearing the one he got at the local jumble sale, for example). Better still, pick something that has a story attached to it: a Jim Thompson label— "I got it in Bangkok after we trekked down from Burma in '99"—is better by far than something grand sounding but for sale in every major store.

In addition to major influences like those above, there are a host of minor issues to worry and decide about as well. Do you put a handkerchief in your top jacket pocket? Well, it is certainly classier looking than a row of pens but could it be a touch old-fashioned? Should your wristwatch look as if no one could land a jumbo-jet or sail round Cape Horn without one? If so, what help is it supposed to have in the buying department? Or is purchasing or financing better done after checking the altitude and humidity? Should you have your hair cut a bit? Or have the grey bits touched out just a little, or a touch of grey added to give an impression of mature judgement? Overall, it is no doubt best to play it safe to avoid any hint of non-conformity or eccentricity. On the other hand, some successful people do have a touch of uniqueness—an individuality that cuts them out from the rest. The truly successful people have some style—a style that sits comfortably on them. And, as Louis Armstrong said about jazz—*if you have to ask what that is, you will never recognise it.*

66A well tied tie is the first serious step in life.99

Oscar Wilde

Some of the above, of course, apply equally to men and women. Dirty shoes spoil anyone's overall look. But there are other considerations. Women have more flexibility as to how they dress, with nothing like the norm of men's suit and tie to follow. This flexibility and range of choice can make it even more difficult to play it just right. Some things, like whether a plunging neckline and accompanying cleavage, will get you into the Boardroom or into trouble (or perhaps both—in reverse order) have become a cliché. Other things, like how much jewellery or make-up to wear, rightly or wrongly, are likely to typecast any woman who gets them wrong.

Perhaps it is easier for a man.

Overheard:

First secretary: "Doesn't Mr. Lee dress well?"
Second secretary: "Yes, and so quickly!"

Easy or not to get it right, personal appearance certainly matters. Just one item out of place and the focus of attention is on that item rather than on the overall good image. So think carefully about how you are likely to be perceived and seek to balance the effect. It may be better to achieve the impression you want, bearing in mind who it is that you wish to impress rather than be regarded as being at the leading edge of fashion.

It is not just how you yourself look but what you have with you and around you that produces the total effect. Which trappings of office life you choose to surround yourself with will contribute just as much to peoples' view of you as you yourself do. Everything, from your mobile phone and the fountain pen with which you no doubt sign your letters, to the car in which you arrive at the office, says something about you. Because it is so disproportionately important, we will consider the car first.

Last year's model

There can be little doubt that the most emotive thing in the whole of corporate life is the company car. Stand quietly in an office 100 metres from where the company accountant (or whoever has drawn the short straw and administers the scheme) sits and whisper 'company car' under your breath and, in many companies, you will hear 'them' scream.

No one, but no one, is ever happy with the car they have at the moment. It is either a 'not a good enough' model, or it is the wrong colour. It is a Saloon when you want an Estate, or vice versa. It does not have the sunroof or some other essential bolt-on-goodie that you have your heart set on, or it has the wrong badge on the back. Even when people are allowed to choose which car they have, up to a certain value for example, it is still never quite right. This fact is compounded by the marketing approach taken by most motor companies. This ensures that six weeks or six months after your gleaming new car is delivered, whatever model it is, it is revised or superseded in a way that makes yours look immediately dated for the rest of its life with you.

The fact that the car gets you from A to B, that it is probably very much better than any car you would buy for yourself, that it is insured and serviced for you and is a real financial perk seems to have little or no bearing on the matter. Except, of course, with those people who do not qualify for a car and who see all the advantages easily enough. The way in which allocation works in many companies hardly helps. Those who actually spend their lives in their cars, like sales people, are doing 60,000 miles a year in a bog-standard L-model Ford, while managers who never get out of the office during the working day have plush Volvos or BMWs sitting in the company car park.

Some curious selection goes on when choice is permitted and, there are those people who are clearly using the car to make a point. A particular choice may say someone is 'green', practical, reliving his or her lost youth or, demonstrated by the whole look of it, either the stage of life he or she is at (a car full of baby seats and assorted paraphernalia, for instance) or his or her perfectionism (not a speck of mud, whatever the season).

If you do not, as yet, have a company car, do not despair. Seek out tasks which, however peripheral to your job, make travel essential. Study the grading schemes within the organisation to see where you fit in, how you can claim some form of comparability with those who do not have cars. Until the rising tax on company cars changes the situation radically, there will always be friction about this matter. Even when you succeed, when you finally have one, there is then the question of where on earth you park it, and who pays the fines if you park somewhere you should not.

Meantime, if you have to drive your own car, choose carefully. If it is too old and decrepit, others may think you care nothing for such things. If it is too smart, they will think you do not need a company one or that you have a private income or a hand in the till.

> 66 Take most people, they're crazy about cars... I don't even like old cars. I mean they don't even interest me. I'd rather have a goddamn horse. A horse is at least human for God's sake. 99
>
> *J. D. Salinger*

Megalomania Case No 2: *Lessons can be expensive*
There are those who would not see an opportunity if it jumped up and bit them on the bottom. There are those who grab opportunities with open hands, and those who grab them…with protective gloves.

Colin Kerr was flattered when the Chairman asked him to investigate, set out and report to the Board with a plan recommending which areas of the office should be made 'no smoking' zones. After all, he had never personally had a slot to speak at a Board meeting before. It was a contentious issue. It would need careful handling but,—in a world increasingly concerned with health, the environment and conservation—it seemed not a bad thing to be associated with. Colin went to work with a will. He canvassed opinions. He checked out the attitude of other firms. He looked into the practical implications—increased hygiene in the kitchen, lower cleaning costs and so on—and prepared his case. He put this into a carefully drafted report, and rehearsed the way he would present it at the meeting. His recommendation, with some carefully chosen exceptions, was to make most of the office a smoke-free zone.

At the Board meeting he had been asked to attend, his report caused considerable lack of agreement. Opinions flew to and fro, through the thickening cigar smoke, and when a vote was taken—stalemate. Colin was amazed when the Chairman's vote was against the plan—after all, he had asked for the policy to be reviewed in the first place.

The revised, compromise plan Colin was asked to issue succeeded only in alienating almost everyone. Smokers thought it was too much; non-smokers thought it was too little. The Chairman thought such a policy was much better associated with Colin than with himself and noted that few, if any, of those areas to be designated 'non-smoking' were places he often visited. "Must watch that Colin," he said to himself "he has the makings of a first class scapegoat." He made a note in his diary that he might be the very person to head the I. T. committee...until it was disbanded? Next year.

Moral: Opportunities offered from above may not be all they seem. The more senior people in the organisation may not be the best politicians but they cannot be underestimated—what with too much experience and success they have usually had.

Bits and bobs

What do you notice when you go into someone's office? There is the size and general ambience, the desk and other furniture, the overall feel of purposeful organisation or unruly chaos but then, having taken in the large scale and obvious features, you begin to notice the detail. Little things catch your eye as you glance round, more so as you gaze round trying to while away another interminable meeting. In such circumstances you will often count the cracks in the wall to dispel boredom, never mind taking in more obvious details. The little things say a great deal about people. They help build a picture so you need to consider what you have around that will catch the eye of other people. What exactly should you have around? What should you avoid? What do you avoid because it tells people at once that they are in the presence of an executive wimp or habitual loser? Some things are clearly right or wrong, others are difficult to define, and there can be a fine line between things that help to build the right image and those that give the wrong impression.

> 66 If all else fails, immortality can always be assured by spectacular error. 99
> *Professor J K Galbraith*

For instance take tidiness, or the reverse; even this has to be carefully judged. Too many heaped in-trays, scattered papers and yellow 'post-it' notes stuck on every available surface may shout chaos and incompetence rather than power and authority. On the other hand, a completely clear desk at the end of the day may look too good to be true, and suggest you have nothing of any real importance to do. Besides, this is almost impossible to achieve.

There can be an endless list of items for the office. But first, here are some examples of things that may be placed on the desk:

- A *clock* of itself may seem fussy or unnecessary, but one with a world time function may say 'jet-setter'—or look pretentious.

- A *presentation pen set* can look classy—best of all if there is a good inscription on it, or a story to go with it—"When I concluded that big deal at the Chicago conference..."

- *Photos* must be carefully selected—of the family perhaps, especially when your wife is 20 years younger than you and looks like a film star. Do not display a photograph of some random beauty and then say it is your wife's. The truth will all come out in the end and your wife will be high on the list of those with something to say about it! You can display photos of significant events—you speaking at the annual conference as Chairman of the Trade Association perhaps—but do not overdo it. Also, do not include a picture of Britain's Duke of Edinburgh or of Bill Gates, unless you have really been introduced to him.

- *Executive games*—the kind that rolls stainless steel balls into different positions to aid decision making, is really not 'on'. People may think that it is the way you actually do make your decisions, and at worst they may think it explains some of them!

- *Newspapers* can show you keep up with events, either in the city or in other peoples' bedrooms, depending on which paper you favour. The pink international edition of the *Financial Times* is a good one and being coloured, it is obviously nice. If you do not want the expense of buying it every day, then buy Saturday's edition (which is, in any case, an excellent read) and leave it on view all week.

- *Ashtrays* (and the whole subject of smoking) these days are an interesting and to a degree, vexed topic. Some people keep them spotlessly clean, just for visitors. Others keep them hidden, only producing them for selected visitors (after all the Managing Director may smoke). In every case, they need to be large enough and preferably should have an enigmatic logo on them hinting that there is some story behind their being in the office at all. If you smoke yourself, do empty the wretched things regularly; if you do not, then there will be many occasions when you can effortlessly make any visitor who does smoke uncomfortable just by declaring your office a 'no smoking' zone. In various countries, there are laws forbidding smoking in offices now.
- *Telephones* are essential. Your office will need one, perhaps two (external and internal) but no more. You only need a third, especially a red one, if the Russian President really does call you regularly.

Overheard:

> ❗ "The only thing more impressive than answering the phone in the car, is to ⬤ have your secretary answer and say, "Hold on, he's on the other line".

- A *calendar* is acceptable, if only so that you know what day of the week it is. An old Pirelli one remains a status symbol—and colleagues may be confused by the fact that all the days of the week will not match the dates.

- A *'Filofax'* organiser still seems to imply efficiency and good organisation but make sure it is a real one, and keep it safe; it will doubtlessly contain intimate details of your whole life, so losing it is rather like losing a limb. Ditto a PDA.

- *Work-in-progress* should be in evidence. Add to the pile anything that appears right in your environment— piles of computer print out may either look good or as if you are collecting waste paper for recycling. So choose carefully.

- A *computer* is always a good thing to have around, especially if it is a smart laptop. It will, however, be impressive only if people think you can 'work' it. Some people may not wish to shatter the illusion by actually switching it on.

Overheard:

> **!** From an IT specialist asked to define the term 'user-friendly': "It actually **●** means it is very complicated, but not as complicated as next year's model will be."

One could add to such a list small items such as a range of suitably impressive reminder notes—'Ring stockbroker re: share tip', implying inside information and money beyond your salary. 'Book table at the Institute of Directors for lunch with S', implying that you move in high circles and making them wonder, "Who's S?"

Next, cast your thoughts wider than the desk. What else is there, or should be there around your office?

- A *notice board* is always a good idea. Just as most of us must touch what is signed as 'wet paint' just to check, everyone must glance at what you have pinned on the wall. You can decide what people see, and make sure it intrigues, puzzles or worries them.
- *Books*—an essential indication of some degree of intelligence—must be carefully chosen. They are commented on in detail later, see 'Read on'.
- *Certificates* can be impressive or speak of past glories. Too far past and it seems like ancient history. So if the only one you have is from a short course you attended 15 years ago—forget it.
- *Luggage labels* are favoured by some. Look out for hotels and travel companies who supply them free, especially if they are classy leather ones. They are useful for making an impression—"When did he go there?"—but only, of course, if they are from the likes of the St. Pierre in New York or The Oriental in Bangkok. One from an undistinguished commercial hotel in some place no one has ever heard of will not have the same cache, though it may still stop your luggage from being lost next time you approach the vagaries of many an airport.
- *Anything exclusive* particularly if people are going to

wonder however you got hold of it. Even something like your own coffee pot will achieve this effect especially when everyone else has to make do with the indifferent brew provided by an aged machine three floors up.

All sorts of things can display a message. The decorated mug from which you drink your tea or coffee may speak volumes. A spare suit on the back of the office door may hint at important evening functions to attend, or may mean that you arrive at the office in a tracksuit, by bicycle. Both may intrigue. Look at your surroundings therefore, ask yourself what needs to be cleared up, added, removed or otherwise revised to correspond with or enhance your chosen image. Whatever you surround yourself with will say something about you. Make sure it is the right thing though.

As a final example, I saw a business card recently. It was smartly designed and comparatively conventional, except that, on the reverse, it said, "Other numbers you might find useful". This was followed by a list of business leaders and famous business *gurus*. I do not know whether the phone numbers were genuine or not—maybe it would only be a clever idea if they were.

66 You can fool too many of the people too much of the time. 99

James Thurber

Finally, you should be beware of panaceas. There is no one thing that will transform or guarantee that you project the image you want, only the cumulative effect of a number of different things can do that—and you have to work at cultivating the image you want.

How well you communicate contributes greatly to the image you want to create and project. After all, you cannot sit around all day just *looking* impressive. You may actually have to say something from time to time. And, as we will see next, communication around an organisation is a little more complicated than that needed to say "Hello" or "Mine's a gin and tonic."

Key guidelines to success

- *You only get one chance to make a good first impression.* This is very important. It must not be underrated. First impressions count. First impressions last—and second impressions could do just as much—perhaps more.

- *Be consistent.* Having decided how you want to be seen, having begun to cultivate a positive image, stick with it. If you chop and change with the wind, those you seek to have an impact on will simply become confused.

- *It pays to advertise.* Remember, no one may sing your praises if you do not do so. The successful office politician is visible (this does not imply that nothing should be done behind the scenes—quite the reverse, but unless you are seen to be a power in the land, you will not achieve as much).

- *Perception is reality.* You can only ever be as influential as you are *seen* to be.

03

The Power of Performance

Even the most astute organisational politicians need to do some work if they are to succeed. And work itself is not enough. It is wisely said that you should never confuse activity with achievement. You have to be seen to be delivering. Indeed, one aspect of what office politics is about is maximising the effect your achievements have on your position and progress. Another is probably covering for a lack of achievement, but even a master politician cannot do that forever. To be able to perform you need to:

- have clear objectives
- have the right skills
- use time productively
- do the things that matter (and not prevaricate)

Putting yourself in a position to fulfil all these criteria may take some politicking so let us look at these areas one by one.

66 Beware of making five-year projections, unless you're thinking of leaving the organisation within four years. 99

Stan Wilson

If you don't know where you are going…

Whatever you do, you must have some direction. It is one of the oldest and wisest management maxims around that 'if you don't know where you are going, any road will do' and certainly, the late Peter Drucker coined such a phrase in one of his early books.

The same sentiment is put, rather differently and in a form that may help the memory, in Lewis Carroll's childhood classic *Alice through the Looking Glass*. Here, Alice is talking with the Cheshire Cat:

> "Would you tell me, please, which way I ought to go from here?"
> *"That depends a good deal on where you want to get to,"* said the Cat.
> "I don't much care where…" said Alice.
> *"Then it doesn't matter which way you go,"* said the Cat.
> "…so long as I get somewhere," Alice added as an explanation.
> *"Oh, you're sure to do that,"* said the Cat, *"if only you walk long enough."*

The fact remains: without clear intentions, you are not only likely to be in a mess but will have no way of measuring how you are doing too. Plans pervade organisational life. You may well need a personal plan and have personal targets to hit; you may be involved in a departmental or functional plan, say the marketing plan, and have targets linked to that too. Despite the fact that some define planning as anticipating the inevitable and then taking the credit for it, there is serious purpose here. A plan focuses and directs activity. It is as important sometimes to use a plan to rule out what you will not do as it is to set out what must be done—and ultimately, a plan must have action plan connotations. It must say who will do what and when it will be done.

Plan your work and work the plan—good advice. Indeed, this is true of any plan, including your personal or career plan on how to survive and thrive in the corporate environment. You need to know what you can try or have to do say, to get a seat on the Board or whatever. No plan should be a straightjacket, however. A plan needs to be flexible, to spell out—with some accuracy—the manageable future say, the next year, and to give a broad indication as to what follows. As time goes by, you can adjust the plan to ensure that details are filled in and that it continues to reflect reality. There is all the difference in the world between an overoptimistic hope and a real plan with some possibility of what it says being achieved. That said, always aim high—anyway, you can, if necessary, adjust your aspirations back. If you do not aim high you may simply end up settling for second best by default.

Once upon a time...

A classic tale is of some relevance here.

> *A medieval King, with his entourage, is crossing the forest on a hunting trip. On a series of trees they see a painted target and in the exact centre of each, there is an arrow. "What incredible accuracy," says the King. "We must find the archer."*
>
> *Further on they catch up with a small boy carrying a bow and arrow. He is frightened at being stopped by the King's party, but admits that he fired the arrows. "You did shoot the arrows, didn't you?" queried the King. "You didn't just stick them into the targets by hand?" The boy replies, "Your majesty, I swear I shot all the arrows from a hundred paces". "Incredible," said the King. "You must accept a job at the palace, I must have an archer of such brilliance near me. But tell me, you are so young, how do you achieve such accuracy?"*
>
> *The boy looked sheepish. "Well," he said, "first I step out a hundred paces, then I fire the arrow into the tree... and then I walk back and paint the target on the tree."*

A bad workman

There is an old saying that 'a bad workman blames his tools'. He is convinced he is not the cause of any failure: so with tools, with skills. If you thought you got a business qualification of some sort and then ruled a line under 'learning', then think again. Somebody coined the term 'lifetime learning' for a reason. Any job demands that whoever does it has a variety of skills. This may be technical say, in aspects of communication or management, and doubtlessly include a variety of specific skills, some of them touched on within these pages, such as the ability to make a good presentation or write a clear report. In a dynamic world, many such skills change and need to be refreshed or enhanced; and new ones come along, worthy of being added to your list too. Some skills are reasonably fixed—I can type fast enough for the writing work I do and doing it keeps up my speed. I had to spend some time and then practice, some years back, to get going but provided that the qwerty keyboard continues to be the standard, and no one truly perfects dictating software, I should not have to do too much more about it.

Other skills—and in my experience these include many connected to the computer (and I really must learn how to … sorry, digressing again)—seem to need attention in some way on a daily basis. You will only succeed by consciously ensuring that you can do whatever portfolio of things you need to be able to do, and can do them well though there are other things to be thought about too. If you cannot do something, who can? And are they prepared to do it for you? Some people swap tasks: you read and check my proofs and I turn your deathless prose into something that might actually impress your readers. Others seem to have a variety of acolytes happy to do their bidding.

While you do not need to be able to lay eggs to be a chicken farmer, you may well benefit from looking fairly widely at the skills in play around you and deciding which of them you must actually be able to undertake and to what level. Whatever must be involved, decide and do it—your political skills need to sit alongside other work skills. All together, they can help you make progress.

Time is relative

Not only does the work you do take time, so does any politicking you deploy too. Good time management is essential: it can enhance productivity, focus you on priorities and act directly to improve your effectiveness. Certainly, you will notice that some people are better organised than others—and see how they benefit from it. Time is a common resource. Unless there are creatures near Alpha Centuri flexing their tentacles to their work 28 hours in their day, everyone everywhere has the same 24-hour day to work with. Some of that time should be reserved too—for eating, sleeping, having sex and listening to Miles Davis (or Oasis I suppose, but please do it where I cannot hear). Everyone is concerned with work/life balance these days. The work bit needs some real organisation to keep it in proportion.

66 Time is more valuable than money. You can get more money, but you cannot get more time. **99**

Jim Roan

It is difficult to achieve what you want when you exist in chaos, your desk is hidden below stacks of paper and your most repeated remark is, "When was it you wanted it?"

Incidentally, what is 'procrastination' exactly? There are probably many stories that can be used to define the concept, but I like this one:

A man is lying very ill in hospital. The doctors come and go, specialists are sent for, but no clue is discovered as to what the cause of his illness is. More tests are done, so many that his life becomes a routine: a test one day, the results a week later, then another test and another wait for the result. But there is still no cause discovered for his sickness. Then one Friday, a doctor comes in and tells him, "At last we know what's wrong with you. But I'm afraid there is some bad news—and also some very bad news—which do you want first?" The man struggles to answer. "Let's have the bad news," he says. "Well, I'm afraid one of the tests shows that you only have one week to live," says the doctor. "My God," says the man, "in that case, what on earth is the very bad news?"

The doctor looked embarrassed: "Well, we got the test result in last Thursday," he said, "and, err ... but we couldn't bear to tell you."

And that is certainly procrastination.

You can tell this story to your more disorganised colleagues. Do not put it off, tell them now.

Yet there are inherent difficulties involved. Few people are perfect time managers. But what makes a difficult task easier? The key is adopting the right attitude towards the process, seeing it as something to work at, one where details matter and the time implications of everything must be—and are—considered.

Not easy, but a conscientious effort to change can ensure good practice quickly becomes habit and thus, things get progressively easier.

It was said earlier that you should 'plan the work and work the plan'. Consider the 'work the plan' bit—the right principles are not complex. Three main ones are to:

- list the tasks you have to perform
- assign them priorities
- do what the plan says

The last two certainly cause problems. However, it is useful to categorise tasks say, grouping telephone calls together. Similarly, allocate time for tasks just as you schedule appointments and balance key areas such as planning and implementation. The 'urgent' must not predominate, especially when its urgency is questionable—some things are truly important. A fundamental principle of time management is—investing time now to save time later. Take a personal example, that of job applications: tailoring your CV and writing an original cover letter takes some time. But initiating contact with another prospective employer, if an approach nosedives through a lack of precision due to lack of preparation, takes longer—much longer.

You must aim to stay 'on plan'. Three main influences conspire against completing planned tasks. These are: other people, events and you. First, you—you may delay action because you:

- are of unsure what to do
- dislike the task
- prefer another task (despite the clear priority)
- fear the consequences, etc

or, simply because the 'bits' keep mounting up and overpower you, or provide an excuse. Additionally, how much time do you waste spending too long on things not because they are important but because you *like* doing them? Be honest. Often, a major timewaster, this dilutes a focus on priorities. Remember: poorly handled regular tasks waste more time than one off ones. A modern indulgence is taking time to check for new 'important' e-mails every five minutes. Certainly, principles need noting, like the fallacy that problems get easier if delayed. Rather, the reverse is true: things put off get more difficult to tackle. So taking prompt action where appropriate can save time.

In an organisation, colleagues interrupting and saying,—"Got a minute?"—can mean that an hour or more vanishes unconstructively. Sometimes, saying a firm "No" is inherent to good time management; and sometimes it needs to be said as "NO!" Likewise, ringing telephones punctuate our lives but there are moments when we need to be 'unavailable'—some tasks can only be completed in a quiet hour. Constant interruptions make them take longer to do—especially tasks requiring thought or creativity.

Making sure others do not waste your time can be a political act that can change a whole culture. A further thing to bear in mind is the link between time and quality. Perfection is not always necessary—I remember reading in an American book someone bemoaning his lot and saying, *They didn't want it right, they wanted it Wednesday.*

Indeed, good time management gives a real boost to competence. Explore the possibilities, instigate good habits and avoid any dilution of your firm intentions, and the results might surprise you. One classic timewaster can be the ubiquitous meeting—something that is commented on a little later. You need to ensure that you maximise your effective use of time and perhaps, also that, other people are envious of your ability to do so.

Now, another thing about time management … no, sorry, time has run out and we must move on.

66 The trouble with punctuality is that nobody's there to appreciate it. 99

Franklin P Jones

Getting somewhat uncomfortable

Performance does not just happen. The office politicians must ensure that they achieve successful results as a foundation to their activity. In seeking effectiveness, there is an irresistible temptation to search for panaceas, one straightforward approach that will improve or guarantee business results, when realistically such magic formulae are often very well-disguised—as hard work. There are few easy options to make your business life successful. That said, there may be one approach to how you work where attention to it, and resolve about it, *can* positively affect many key activities.

Some things end up, however unintentionally, going by default. To prevent this, you need to be honest about yourself first.

So let me start. Despite being, I like to think, knowledgeable about, and having practiced in various areas of management and business, there are, I admit, some tasks where my approach falters. It is difficult to admit this (damn it, I have written a book about time management![1]) but … I have been known to procrastinate. Occasionally. Where does this happen most often? On examination, it is easy to say: it happens when something is not just difficult (I enjoy a challenge!) but when it is a particular kind of difficult—when it is actually uncomfortable. This may be conscious: for example, there are things about my computer skills that mean action is delayed—I know that certain of my skills are not all they should be and am conscious that it is all too easy to get into deep trouble; one wrong key stroke and—disaster. Everyone probably has things that prompt such thoughts, and so we delay action.

Alternatively, there are things where avoidance is a more subtle process, where we try to rationalise and do not actually accept that our procrastination is significant, sometimes refusing to see the reality at all. As a result, things are left unaddressed and performance can deteriorate directly. And all because of some woolly,

[1] Successful Time Management (Kogan Page).

half-buried and perhaps repressed feeling that taking action will be an uncomfortable experience. Consider the following example.

Imagine: One of your staff is performing under par. This might be anything from not hitting sales targets to poor attendance. The details are unimportant but one thing is clear—it demands action. The rewards are considerable and, let us say, easily recognised. Dealing with the problem will produce more sales, higher productivity—whatever, depending on the precise details. Yet ... with such things there can seem to be so many reasons for delay. We think (or rather hope) that the problem will get better. We wait for other things: the end of the month (bringing further figures or evidence) or a forthcoming appraisal (which we know means we cannot put it off later than that). More than anything, we blame other things. We are busy we say, we have greater priorities or, even less convincingly, we are sorting other problems—fire fighting.

The truth is actually that we do not *want* to deal with the problem. We may be unsure how to do so, and that can be awkward. More likely, we do know what to do but know it will be awkward or embarrassing to do so. Addressing the problem will take us into the *discomfort zone* and we would rather distance ourselves, busying ourselves elsewhere (with something more important!) and remaining safely outside this zone of personal difficulty.

The facts of the matter are usually clear. The problem is not rocket science and we can usually address it if we deal with it. Indeed, a poor performance is a good example. It is important, yet it is not complicated. Essentially, you are left with only three options—you can:

1. Put up with the poor performance, and allow it to continue (which is surely something no one would defend or recommend).
2. Address the problem by being determined to cure it—persuading or motivating your staff to perform better; training or developing them to do their jobs better if poor performance is due to a lack of some skill or competence.
3. Conclude perhaps, after option two has failed, that your staff will never get better and fire them (or otherwise move them to other areas of responsibility).

Both options 2 and 3 may be awkward. It can be embarrassing to tell someone that his or her performance is unacceptable, and most of us would find firing someone worse. So, the result is that action is delayed.

Get real. The situation here needs to be addressed head on. Such a situation is not a failing of logic, not a deficit of information or understanding, or anything else that mistakenly leads us away from the sensible and necessary course—*it is a personal decision: we put avoiding personal discomfort above sorting the problem and, very likely, delay makes the problem worse.*

Before you say—"But I never make that kind of decision"—consider further. If this thinking is partly subconscious, then that is likely so because we push it into the back of our minds, refusing to really analyse what is occurring or simply allowing other activity to create a blinding smokescreen. Now, let us think more constructively. Which elements of our work are likely to run foul of this kind of avoidance technique? Dealing with poor performance has already been cited as an example. Others include:

- *Raising a difficult issue at a meeting* (it gets put off rather than risking controversy or argument)
- *Networking* (sounds good: we all hope to meet people at that conference we attend, then come out with one business card because we are not quite sure how to approach people—Frances Kay has written a book on this subject)
- *Chasing debtors* (we hate it, avoid it or do it half heartedly and so cash flow suffers; yet we all recognise that it is not an order until the money is in the bank)

Such things are, to an extent, routine. Others may be more personal, linking to a particular skill or activity. For instance:

- Avoiding presentations, even when they offer promotional opportunity, because—*It's not really my thing.*
- Avoiding sitting on a committee where you might make valuable contacts because meetings are in the evening and—*It's not fair to the family.*

You may well be able to extend the list in both categories (be honest, as I said at the beginning).

So, what should you conclude from this? There is a significant opportunity here. You need to resolve to *actively seek out uncomfortable situations*. You need to see the *discomfort zone* as an attractive place to go—somewhere where you can achieve action and influence results, and often do so quickly and easily. After all, most people can probably identify with this feeling: you take some long overdue action, find—however momentarily distasteful it may be doing it—that it changes things for the better and end up saying— "I just wish I had done that sooner."

Think about it. Identify areas where this phenomenon can strike. Do so systematically and make this a habit. Make *entering the discomfort zone* a catchphrase. This approach is the antidote to things going by default. It needs some resolve, but here is truly a technique which, overriding an undesirable element of human nature, provides a simple, sure way to increase your effectiveness. Now I have been using writing this section as an excuse for long enough, I must go and … be masochistic.

04

Communication

Nothing much happens without some communication taking place. Communication oils the wheels of the organisation and on occasion, puts sand in the gears too. It presents some problems, but is a source of many opportunities too. Thus, the successful office politician takes communication very seriously.

> **"**It is always the best policy to tell the truth, unless, of course, you are an exceptional liar.**"**
> *Jerome K Jerome*

Megalomania Case No 3: *Musical chairs*
With the resignation of the Marketing Director, Julian Grimes had to sort something out. He was the Finance Director and knew nothing about marketing, but the reorganisation necessary now needed a firm decision at Board level and he seemed to draw the short straw with regards to it.

Of the three other key personnel in the section, the Marketing Manager was also moving on and the other two, a Marketing Executive and an Assistant were both comparatively new and junior. Julian did not really know either of them.

He consulted with the Director and Manager. Neither was, in fact, interested, being more concerned with their own futures. If Mary, the Manager, could land the Director's job though, she might be interested in staying on. Her recommendations naturally described the configuration of the senior job in a way that played to her strengths.

Julian was sure of little, but it seemed to him that an outsider in the top job would sort out the differences best, or at least, without his having to referee. He therefore drew up the job descriptions for the reconfigured department and circulated it in the organisation in a way that appeared to change the exact nature of all four jobs. The effect was such as to make life, and the likely marketing success of the company, more difficult. The Director was out of it anyway. Mary saw that she had no chance of the top job, accepted the offer she had been sitting on and handed in her resignation.

The other two, un-consulted and uncertain as to their future, resolved to look around for another job as fast as possible. After all, as one said to the other, "... with this lack of concern for the department, what chance is there of them appointing someone really good to do the top job."

> <u>Moral</u>: Communication is about people. You have to carry the people with you, whether the news for them is good or not. Change will not happen smoothly unless people are committed to it. Julian sought to deal with a sensitive and important issue without consultation, presumably believing that he would get it off his plate soonest that way. He ended up upsetting everyone, jeopardizing the ongoing results needed from the department concerned and, no doubt, making his own life more complicated in the process.

Now, if you *really want* to upset everyone, lack of consultation and bold unconsidered announcements may be just the right tactic ... but that is another matter.

I say ... I say ... I say ...

Most of what goes on in the office is communication. We communicate with colleagues, with subordinates, with our staff, with our bosses, with those inside and outside the organisation. We do so face to face, in writing, over the telephone and in a variety of different ways—from e-mail to loud shouts across the open office. Communication is so important that if you were to remove it from office life, not a great deal would happen at all.

Of all the things that do go on in the organisation, communication is surely, and without doubt, the simplest. Other things are complicated. Working the photocopier when you want it to print both sides of the paper is complicated. Filling in the form you need before a capital purchase is approved is complicated. And plucking up the courage to ask the boss for a raise in salary or an extra day off around the next public holiday is downright difficult. Communicating on the other hand—just telling people things—is easy. Or is it? When was the last time you said, "But I'm sure you said ..." When was the last time you were asked, "What exactly do you mean?" When was the last time you were involved in a communications breakdown; and when was it that what happened was bad enough to be categorised as an 'out and derailment'?

There are many classic stories that illustrate the problems of communication. Years ago a businessman telexed his office in New York from South Africa asking whether he should buy diamonds. The reply came back—"NO PRICE TOO HIGH"—and he duly bought. A week later, thrown out on his ear because of the losses that had been made, he reflected on the difference a full stop would have made. The reply should have read "NO <u>STOP</u> PRICE TOO HIGH." Similar but perhaps differently motivated to the reply a journalist, researching a show business feature, received having cabled Hollywood "HOW OLD CARY GRANT?" it said "OLD CARY GRANT FINE <u>STOP</u> HOW YOU?" Such confusion is no less likely today as many people send highly abbreviated text messages on their mobile phones. In the rush and bustle of a busy office, in our haste to get things done, it is all too easy for misunderstandings of this sort to occur. For whatever reason, what is said—or written or transferred in some other way—gets misunderstood and sometimes, if something is ambiguous, an opportunity is grabbed and it is intentionally misunderstood. Indeed, many of the problems that crop up from time to time in any organisation have as their root cause, poor communication. So communication skill is vital in office life, and this key skill is similarly necessary for those people intent on scoring a few points and getting a step ahead.

The problem is further confounded by the fact that often surprisingly, people deliberately misunderstand— perhaps because they do not want to do or are not sure how to do something.

> 66 Get your facts first and then you can distort them as much as you wish. 99
>
> *Mark Twain*

In addition to the inherent problems described—cropping up perhaps because people are not thinking, or are making assumptions, or are just not listening—there are other factors to be considered. Apart from those people with no political aspirations—a breed as rare as the dodo or hen's teeth it has to be said—whose communications will be straightforward, if not always crystal clear, other people will lay certain political overtones on much of what they say. This just adds to the inherent difficulties of clear communication. These overtones can be graded in three strengths. Those that are:

- *Devious*—In these communications, some additional message lurks, usually something that will help the sender later.

- *Very devious*—In these, there are more layers of meaning than an onion.
- *Downright Machiavellian*—Unravel these communications if you can and whilst you try—watch your back.

Incidentally Machiavelli,—Niccolo Machiavelli that is—the archetypal devious diplomat who years ago gave his name to the phrase 'Old Nick' to describe the devil, is the same person who, more recently, also gave his name to the phrase 'Management by Machiavelli'. This phrase is now regularly used to describe anything that is more underhand than perhaps it should be.

A touch of deviousness is perhaps something to which everyone resorts occasionally. Being economical with the truth—as it is called these days—to the extent of telling the truth selectively or omitting some key element of the full story, has become almost normal practice. In the political arena it is endemic, no apology seems to be made for it and it even has its own name: 'spin'. What about the ethicality of using an out and out lie? When is it—is it ever—ethical to have even a momentary mouthful of truth decay?

Some people take the view that lying is completely immoral. You cannot, after all, get 8 out of 10 for honesty. Something is either a lie or not. Though I have seen company appraisal systems that do measure honesty,—this seems nonsensical—surely such a system would mark you either honest or fired! Sorry, I digress. Conversely, many people believe lies can be extremely useful. For some of these people, 'ethical' is not a word that appears in their business dictionary. The trouble is that one lie tends to lead to another—and another—and this not only taxes the memory, it usually leads to discovery.

So when you open your mouth to say something, make sure that you are not putting your foot in it. A "No" when you mean "Yes", or a "Yes" when you mean "Maybe", could be all it takes to collapse the carefully built facade of your image. Any building needs good foundations, particularly one that is reaching for the heights. Similarly with people— it is worth making sure that you put substance into this element of your position.

Ten phrases that (probably) indicate a lie

- "I can honestly say…"
- "I'm not interested in speculation, but…"
- "I'm very sympathetic to…"
- "This is really interesting…"
- "I have it on good authority that…"
- "Believe me when I say…"
- "The truth is…"

And, classically:

- "The computer will sort it out…"
- "The cheque is in the post…"
- "Of course, I will still love you in the morning."

A little deviousness, however, is perhaps another matter. Can that do no harm? Perhaps not. Indeed, adding a touch of guile to the way you go about things may make the difference between success and failure.

Adding any touch of deviousness to your own communications always needs a degree of finesse, and it sits more effectively on a good and sound communication than on one that is muddled, unthought of or simply unclear. So an ability to communicate, preferably a more effective one than those around you have, is one of the base stock-in-trades of the office politician. As the old military adage goes: "Ready, aim, fire!" In other words, work out what you are trying to achieve for yourself, line up the best way of getting the message over clearly and then, communicate. Curiously, this works better than any other sequence, particularly one commencing with "Fire!"

Like nailing jam to the wall

Communication is made more difficult by a variety of factors that act as filters between the sender and the receiver of any message. You will regularly have to contend with the effects of prejudice ("I've never believed it can be done that way, and I don't intend to change now"), assumption ("Of course we will use the standard system..."), and sheer inattention ("What?"). But it is no good pleading the pig-ignorance of others as an excuse for your own bad communication. You have to work with all these just to get one clear message over, never mind adding in a degree of subterfuge so all the tricks of the trade will help. To make your communications achieve what you want, you need to watch for (and sometimes use) the following:

- *Exaggeration*

  Though this can, if used to excess, remove all credibility from what you say. On the other hand, if you hide your light under a bushel and fail to blow your own trumpet occasionally, then little recognition will follow. Used in moderation,—some people are greatly in favour of moderation, and use it all the time—it is truly the most useful, indeed perhaps the best possible method of... but we must not overdo a good thing. Enough.

- *Flattery*

  This is also something that must be used carefully, but there is a truth in the old saying that 'a little goes a long way', so do not neglect it as a technique. Do not forget that whilst you would spot it a mile off and treat it with the contempt it deserves, others may not have the same perception. (Note: If in reading the last sentence you have just said to yourself, "That's right I would spot it," then you have proven the point—you are susceptible to flattery. And so too are most people).

- *Generalities and vagueness*

  These can so easily creep into so much of what is said. What is '24-hour service' other than not sufficiently precise? What do we mean when we say, "Leave it with me" or "I will see to it at once"? Any woolliness, that is imprecision of thinking or expression that creeps into communication, is well ... sort of, that is it will, or at least might, give the wrong or anyway a perhaps biased or maybe, inaccurate impression. You see what I mean?

- *Egocentricity*

  Describes any phrase that starts your point of view: "I think ..." "It is my opinion that ..." "My advice is ..."— all these are very different to phrasing things the other way round, as in "Don't you think ..." which focuses on the other person.

- *Big words*

  Rather than impress, *big words* are more likely to be seen as pompous or condescending, or to induce 'pandiculation'[1]. If you want to point out this danger to other people, tell them to avoid 'sesquipedalians': an appropriately long word meaning 'over long words'. But, as they say, never be condescending to people ... You do know what 'condescending' means, don't you?

- *Precision of language*

  This is important too. You may only get one chance to have your say, so make sure the sense of what you mean is clear. It is no good to moan later that someone should have done what you meant, not what you said.

66 I know that you understand what you think I said, but I am not sure that you realise that what you heard is not what I meant. 99

Attributed to the late Richard Nixon

---

[1] The word *pandiculation* describes the act of yawning—a sufficiently exciting piece of information to engender just that.

These, and a dozen other factors, are important if you are to get one message across, even more so if you are to add a few important subtleties as well. Same goes with listening. This may seem obvious, but listening is, in fact, a skill—there are training courses on active listening—and it is certainly a skill that is necessary to the budding office politician. It is one thing to ignore what you hear, quite another not to know what it is you are ignoring. You need to work at listening and above all, you need to read between the lines. The following examples of political 'officespeak' show clearly that what is said is often not what it seems.

Ten examples of "officespeak" (and how to interpret them)

- "I wish I could help." (I could, but I won't.)
- "I'm not one to tell tales." (I will tell everyone.)
- "It's no trouble at all." (I will do it, but regard yourself as in my debt, because actually I do regard it as trouble.)
- "I am sure no one will notice." (I will make sure they do.)
- "Don't worry about it." (Start worrying the moment I walk out of the room.)
- "With great respect." (Actually with no respect at all.)
- "This is no criticism of you." (Not much it isn't—listen up.)
- "Have you a minute?" (Expect a minimum of four hours of interruption.)

- "It is only an idea." (God help you if you do not use it.)
- "I have your best interests at heart." (If you believe that, then I shall promptly sell you London's Tower Bridge. I have my interests at heart.)

A useful body of knowledge

A major amount of information is conveyed non-verbally through a plethora of expressions or gestures whose meanings are, in fact, clear—the withering look that seems likely to bore holes in steel filing cabinets, the sanctimonious smile that says, "I told you so," the raised hand that says, "Interrupt now at your peril". This sort of thing is described by the somewhat inexact science of body language.

For all its imprecision, this is a subject worthy of some study by the political aspirant. The following examples show both how it affects communication and how it can be useful:

- *Space*
  Defined in the late Douglas Adam's *Hitchhiker's Guide to the Galaxy* as "...big. Really big." But, outer space apart, it is the lack of it that causes problems. People like to keep their distance. They have an intimate zone, which is reserved for lovers and children. This expands to a range that is for family and close friends, and which expands further on into a social range. It is in this latter and wider public zone that is where most

business contact occurs, except perhaps that which is transacted out of sight behind the filing cabinets. Get too close to people and you make them feel uneasy; keep them at too much of a distance and they think you are unapproachable.

- *Touching*
  Physical contact is also a sensitive issue. There are some occasions where touching is allowed, even to be recommended, but not so much with 'touching up'. But that is another issue. (You will have to wait for the sequel to this book, an as yet untitled volume about sexual harassment in the office, which seems to be stuck in a lengthy research phase that may well act to delay it indefinitely.)

  Slapping someone on the back is rarely to be recommended especially when the person slapped is more senior. A hand say, on the arm, is more often allowed, but an arm around the shoulders may be misunderstood. The best approach is probably to avoid anything of which you are not absolutely sure. The one regular form of contact that takes place between both sexes, between all levels and kinds of people around the organisation is the handshake. A handshake can still say a lot about you. "Avoid giving a 'wet-fish' handshake because it gives a bad impression of you", must be one of the most often quoted pieces of advice in the world. Yet you still come across people who do it. Who are the people without the wit to make a naturally wet handshake firm? Is it because they have not heard what it has been taken to imply? Or that they do not care? Perhaps it is simply that they are wet. On the other hand, beware of overdoing the firmness. If the hand you shake is crushed to the point of pain, its owner is unlikely to be impressed. Finally, do not use touch to imply deep friendship that does not exist, especially with members of the opposite sex: it quickly appears embarrassingly contrived and at best, is likely to have the reverse effect to that which you intend. At worst, it will get your face slapped.

* *Eye-contact*

  Another much quoted sign of character. Everybody has a mother who believes that if someone will not look you in the eye, he is not to be trusted. There is some truth to this. Lack of eye contact often implies lack of interest. The trouble is that those wishing to display interest make a point of trying to maintain good eye contact, so it may be unreliable as a sign. Also sometimes, too much eye contact can have a different effect and is one of the quickest ways to make people feel uncomfortable. If you really work at it—touch them too intimately and look at them continuously in the eye—you can invade their personal space. Subjected to these tactics they are likely to break and run. The rumours they spread about you thereafter should be interesting, if far-fetched.

- *Position and posture*

  Two other factors to watch. Indeed this whole area is a minefield of signs and suggestions. For example, folded arms are a sure sign of negative feelings. Someone folding his arms in mid conversation is said to be displaying a specific sign of disagreement, and if you see someone with folded arms and clenched fists, watch out, he may well be on the brink of an explosive outburst. Of course, it could just mean he finds the position comfortable, that the chair that he is sitting on has no arms or that he is surreptitiously scratching his armpits. Similarly, leaning forward towards another person during conversation can mean interest or indicate that he is about to doze off. A hand going to cover the mouth may be an attempt to pass off a lie, or conceal halitosis or an imminent yawn.

- *Eyes and face*

  Both are also important and, as has been said, eye contact is one of the most important of all. A refusal to look the person in the eye always gives the impression of one being shifty; eyes shooting nervously round the room appear likewise. Even a smile can be deceptive, either indicative of friendship or anticipated triumph. Remember the poster (taken from the Peanuts cartoon strip) showing poor Snoopy the dog with half his kennel cut away and the tag line 'Never trust a smiling cat'? Watch your expression and that of other people.

66One should not aim at being possible to understand, but at being impossible to misunderstand.99

Marcus Fabious Quintilian

Sometimes, body language gives an overpowering indication about someone. There is a lovely description of someone (in Peter Mayle's book *A Year in Provence*) which goes like this: 'a man who could give lessons in leering.' No further description is given or needed. The moral of this is first, to read up on body language and keep your eyes open—watch for signs. And second, to assume that everyone else is doing the same, and send confusing signals yourself. If the boss catches you lying back in your chair, with your arms folded, your legs crossed and your eyes closed, tell him that you are practising your body language; but persuade him quickly, before he adopts an aggressive stance and kicks the chair from under you.

You make me feel so...

It may be that in your communications around the organisation, there are occasions when it is very important to you that you come out on top. In such circumstances there are those, it has to be said, who will stoop to any low trick to put their adversaries at a disadvantage—to make them feel uncomfortable. As a slightly bizarre example, one manager I once worked for had a special chair for unwelcome visitors. The front legs of the chair were half an inch shorter than the back. This made people very uncomfortable, but the effect was not so extreme that most could fathom out quite why. As a tactic this was much subtler than aiming the desk lamp at them or sitting them with the sun in their eyes; and it seemed to work, and he swore the 'undesirables' did not linger.

Some people seem to unerringly catch you at a bad moment say, when you are already late for another meeting or have just arrived in the office soaking wet from the rain. They raise seemingly unimportant things when you have major issues on your mind. They slip things onto meeting agendas at the last minute, hoping for a decision by default with no real time for discussion. They will stoop to anything, in fact, from forgetting your name to drawing your attention to something you would rather forget, usually something you did not think they knew. This leaves your mind racing through a dozen possible reasons as to why they found out, rather than concentrating on the attack that is being launched on an entirely different topic.

If the opposition is at pains to put you at a disadvantage then not being phased by it is the surest way to win an advantage. You have been asked to give a presentation many miles from your office at 8 o'clock in the morning. You suspect that it has been arranged like that for the sole purpose of making the presentation more difficult because an early start and a difficult journey will precede it. Why should it? It is the same presentation. You have the same amount of time. There is no reason why it should not go well. If those on the receiving end—and let us pretend they are potential clients—expect that you will find it more difficult, that the standard of your presentation skill will suffer, do not give them the satisfaction of seeing such. If you do a first class job despite the difficulties, then you will score extra points. If they are able to say, "Well, he didn't cope with that very well," then you lose; and do so disproportionately. The same principle applies to any similar situation. If you rise above the pressure, whatever it is, then you have the edge. Indeed, it is not always easy. There will be circumstances when you are put on the spot— when the meeting is called at short notice, when you *are* less well prepared than you would like, when the pressure is really on—but one of the skills of winning through is simply to be able to cope, to rise to the occasion.

All these may sound very easy to say, but just *how* do you cultivate such ability? Well, to an extent, it will be there or not, or at least the germ of it will be. For the rest, remember that much apparently ad hoc action—what appears to be a spur of the moment brilliance—is actually carefully planned. As the old military adage goes, 'Time spent in reconnaissance is seldom wasted'. In wartime it stops you getting your head shot off and in the office war, it makes the point that some thought before action is usually to be recommended. So to quote *The Hitchhiker's Guide to the Galaxy* again, "Don't Panic!" Make sure you keep a cool head and rise to the occasion; or rather that you plan to be able to rise to the occasion—and then do so.

66 The secret of success is to offend the greatest number of people. 99

George Bernard Shaw

Round your little finger

If one thing is clear so far from this review, it is surely that there is no short cut to success in office politics. The successful politician makes use of anything and everything that goes on around him. What is more, he regards his adversaries—sorry, friendly rivals—not as a homogeneous group to be dealt with in the same way, but all as individuals needing different tactics. Even so, it helps to regard them as falling into a number of groups, each particular in terms of their awkwardness and how specifically you should deal with them. First let us consider the most difficult types:

- *The 'have a row at all costs' types are just that*—Any little incident is exaggerated and built up into a major row, grudges are very much borne and the end is never heard of almost anything. Because there is no rational grounds for losing their cool, the temptation is to respond to them with rational argument, but this is rather like pouring petrol on a fire—the response is more argument and less rationality. The only way forward with this type of person is to concentrate discussion on the future, and ignore all recriminations about the past. Those who give in to the argument may have a greater battle, they may even win the argument, but only those who bypass this get their way.

- *The 'just-a-minute' types who, given the chance, will keep you talking forever*—They are gossips, they are lonely or isolated, or they simply have verbal diarrhoea. In any case, they are not only great time wasters but will sidetrack you from what you are really trying to do. If they are important to you—good contacts, or potential allies in some way—the danger is that if you do not listen to them, they are offended and any chance of alliance is forfeited. The only tactic here is to use any pause in what they say to bring the topic of conversation back on track. Using a lead-in such as "Now, let's get down to this business of the schedule ..." If you can do this, and yet retain the image of being a good listener, then such a person will be your friend for life.

- *The 'rude-by-nature' types are a little different. Such people are not rude and unpleasant over some incident, however minor. They are just rude about everything and to everyone*—Every organisation has one, and the number seems to increase as manners decline. The danger is that by responding to the rudeness, you make yourself an attractive target. The only way to proceed is to ignore the rudeness, recognise that you will never change them and keep your cool. Keep smiling and then, by refusing to let the process escalate, you will be able to hold some normal communication with them and at least have the satisfaction that you are not letting them get to you.

- *The 'know-it-all' types, who are forever airing their superiority, are also easily rubbed up the wrong way*—They hate having their views challenged and certainly, if you do so and are proven wrong you would be looked down on for a long time. So, if you do challenge such people be sure of your facts. Besides, if they want to feel superior, then to some degree at least, why not let them? A little flattery goes a long way, and may even turn a pain in the neck into an ally. Conversely, you are allowed to adopt the old maxim—'It is those of you who really know it all that really annoy those of us who do'.

- *The 'tongue-tied' types who just will not talk*—They may be nervous, they may be shy but it is the very devil to deal with anyone if there is no response coming back to you. Possibly, if you make it clear that you are there if they want, they will eventually come to you. But you may have an urgent need to draw them into your schemes, in which case the only way to prompt conversation is to ask open-ended questions (those that cannot be answered with "Yes" or "No")—those starting with What? Why? Where? Who? and the like as a way to get them talking. If you persuade them that they can talk to you, and that there is, in fact, no awkwardness about doing so, again you may have more friends for life.

- *The 'double-checker' types who are suspicious—first, second and third—of everything and everybody; who want to check your authority, your reliability, your very soul*—It takes time for these ones, but trust can be built up eventually. Give the answers and details called for, say you will find out, and do, provide chapter and verse and gradually trust will build up, questions decline or abbreviate and again, you can have a friend for life. Uttering one "Why do you need to check that?" too many, however, can quickly provide you with a dangerous enemy.

Of course all these types come in various forms. The senior 'rude-by-nature' types need more careful handling than their more junior counterpart. The useful, or potentially useful, 'tongue-tied' types are worth a degree more patience than those who are not. Remember that, as ever, all is not always as it seems. The silent sort may simply be putting on a front to avoid unnecessary time wasting conversation so that they can get on with a bit of politicking of their own elsewhere.

> **66** I don't want any yes-men around me. I want everyone to tell me the truth even if it costs them their jobs. **99**
>
> *Samuel Goldwyn*

Overheard:

(About the boss)
"You can't help liking the Managing Director—if you don't, he fires you."

(From the boss)
"When I want your opinion, I will give it to you."

As anything and everything that can generally assist your communication—or more specifically give it an edge—may be useful, we will end this section with some examples of how various communications processes can be helpful. First a moment more in the bowels of Megalomania.

Megalomania Case No 4: *Biting your tongue*

The Head of Personnel was regarded by one and all as impossible. Of all the people in the organisation whom one might expect to be people-orientated ... but no, he upsets everyone. Things were vetoed out of hand because it was 'not personnel policy', yet the policy always seemed to be different. Systems that tied everyone else up in paperwork were put in, seemingly to no good purpose. Relations with Training, Administration, even Finance were strained to say the least.

The resultant strains and stresses even affected the Personnel Department itself until at one stormy Heads of Department meeting, the Head of Personnel asked why relations were so difficult. The others present hedged round for some minutes. "Come on," he said to the Administration Manager, "be honest". He was. There was even some tentative agreement around the table, but the meeting ended with nothing resolved and on a more troubled note than usual.

The next meeting was rather different. The new Administration Manager was more circumspect than his recently departed predecessor and the other people present resolved to bide their time.

> Moral: Never speak your mind just because you are
> asked to. In any case, the last thing most people
> usually mean when they say, "Be honest," is for you
> 'to be honest'—especially if they are more senior
> than you are and in charge of some power base. The
> consequences can be dramatic. Shifting the most
> difficult obstructions can rarely, if you are realistic, be
> done on the spur of the moment.

Take a memo

Go into almost any kind of office, open a filing cabinet,
bypassing the external correspondence, with its pleading
letters from unpaid suppliers, complaints from customers
and unopened junk mail, and take a look at the *internal*
documents (of course many of them are e-mails, sent
electronically and never printed out, so you might have to
dip into the computer files too).

There, you will doubtlessly find examples of long
tedious memos padded out to make what should have
been brief, basic points into rambling, interminable essays
of self-importance—those that, as the Americans say,
"uses fifty-cent words to make five-cent points."

You will also find brief, terse, memos.

Others will be protective, accusing or defensive. Some
will be designed to act as insurance—in case something goes
wrong. Others will be informal, some will be
incomprehensible, some will contain jargon, some will be
all jargon. Others will exude smugness— smother their
readers with self-righteousness or condescension (spelling

out their message IN CAPITAL LETTERS, despite being written in upper and lower case). Each will portray—as you read between the lines—something of the personality of their author. They may even reflect something of their writer's state of mind as they wrote, giving clues as to whether each word was laboured over or whether they were on 'automatic pilot' with the pen or typing fingers in gear, but the mind firmly in neutral.

Memos record and address every topic under the sun. They range from claims for expenses (most often filed under fiction) to major treatises on company reorganisation or merger. They can be catalogued by a variety of broad types, of which the top 10 are probably the following:

- *The 'watch-my-lips' memo*—usually from the desk of someone senior, which says either "Do this", or perhaps more politely, "It is only a suggestion, but do bear in mind who is making it." (A favourite approach of some senior people—and not only in memos—this is guaranteed to foster resentment).

- *The 'and-another-thing' memo*—most often dictated, it contains an endless list of disconnected items of no great importance with, just occasionally, some vital point buried,wittingly or unwittingly, in the middle which, of course, nobody notices.

- *The 'for-a-rainy-day' memo*—contains information you are highly unlikely to need but which the writer is, on no account, going to be accused later on of not making available to anyone with the faintest chance of saying "I never saw that" at some time in the future. Having sent such a memo, the writer will never forgive recipients if six months, or indeed, six years later, the information does become relevant and they do not remember or deny receiving it.

- *The 'copies galore' memo*—here, the list of recipients is what matters rather than the content of the memo. This is alternatively called the 'I still exist' memo. This category alone must account for a major percentage of the filing in any organisation—a massive amount of superfluous paper which has to be kept warm in winter, cool in summer and generally takes up space and money to no good effect.

- *The 'information is power' memo*—which is circulated to the smallest number of people so that the memo can be said to exist—"But I sent it to the secondary, back up archive, anyone could have seen it there"—but the information in it actually remains exclusive.

- *The 'keep-off-my-patch' memo*—the memo designed to rather act as the severed heads left impaled on spears by head hunters do along jungle trials, expressly to warn others not to approach. They often start with "It has come to my attention ..."

- *The 'I'm more numerate than you are' memo*—projecting more confusion than sense and more figures at that, this kind is usually accompanied by an inch-thick stack of virtually illegible computer print out. This, in turn, makes the message look more impressive, but probably guarantees it is even less likely to be read.

- *The 'seven years war' memo*—not unlike part-works, one memo following another to build up the case being made relentlessly, though when this is subtly done recipients may well be unaware of what is being worked towards—until it is too late.

- *The 'divide and rule' memo, or rather, memos*—memos, in the plural, because the whole lot consists of several missives, each a little different and sent to a variety of people. Whilst the other categories mentioned can all be used for other purposes, this one is only used for political purposes.

- *The 'come to a meeting' memo*—most of us simply have far too many of this. One reason, of course, is that if you convene a meeting and tell people something, you may be able to avoid writing anything about it at all.

Memos inform yes, but they also confuse, wind-up, overstate or even (often?) misinform. Many people, who would lie through their teeth in conversation if they thought it would help them one tiny jot, will think twice before committing the same thought to writing—they realise that it may come back to haunt them. But this does not mean there is political content in memos. There is not. Be sensible. Look at them long and hard, there may be a message lurking between the lines, or a hidden subtext in that message. Other memos act like a bull at a gate, they constitute straight, undisguised political head-butts.

> 66 A memorandum is written not to inform the reader but to protect the writer. 99
> *Dean Acheson*

Computers, and computer printouts, have already been mentioned. Other forms of technology can help the memo writer further. The dictating machine is the simplest and has been around for a long time, in various forms. These days they are tiny and, whilst the machine will go in the proverbial vest pocket, the memos they produce may need the office equivalent of a forklift truck just to move them from desk to desk. They do, in other words, tend to encourage people to go on a bit. Do not underestimate the skill of dictating, there are some things important enough to be worth the time of drafting carefully. In some cases, several times. Incidentally, a modern alternative to the dictating machine is software that lets you dictate directly to your computer. Such is a wonderful invention: *it al ous ewe to cree ate some frightfully incontinent docu tents*. Oops—back to manual: currently such software allows you to create some virtually incomprehensible documents. Maybe sometimes, that is what you want. However you do it, once your message is down in black and white it may be unalterable. Which brings us to getting things into typed form. Here, no more may be necessary than passing the draft, or tape, to a secretary. But the days of the old manual typewriter have long gone; these days there are other possibilities.

The word processing software in our PCs is a form of technological wizardry that can be extremely useful. (Without them you would probably not be reading this book; but then nothing is perfect.) Not only can word processors make even a sloppy message look smart, they can add a variety of emphasis on their own.

A word processor can put letters and words in place. It can make them bold, to add weight to a point, **bolder**, BOLDER still, or even **BOLDER**. So it can help you say "... this is the case ...", " ... we will NOT do this ..." It can put important points

in boxes.

It can make letters and words large, *fancy*, or very small indeed.

Or it can put

one

word

on

top
of
the
other.

And, of course, a word processor can store things on disc, forever, till hell freezes over or Technical Resources declares that your system is obsolete—which reminds me of the poem:

I bought a new computer
It came completely loaded
It was guaranteed for ninety days
But in thirty was outmoded.

However.

More often, documents stay stored right up until the moment when someone says, "Where can I get a copy of that report?" They may no longer have it, but if you are able to summon it up and produce it nonchalantly, triumphantly or apparently after considerable effort, as the occasion dictates, it may well be useful on occasion.

Thus, it pays to be keyboard literate these days: a posh way of saying you can type using the right fingers for the right keys or are 'qwertified'. Once you have mastered this—a couple of evenings typing such stimulating phrases as:

"The quick brown fox jumped over the lazy dog" and
"I will get this right if it kills me."

should suffice—then you can really get to grips with your word processing system. Most office systems are said to be 'user friendly', which means if you were Space Invaders Champion of 1985, or have studied electronic wizardry with your 12 year-old son, you can probably work it by pure instinct. If, on the other hand, you are an ordinary mortal, you may find doing so somewhat complicated, if only because there seems to be a new system every five minutes. Portable virtual keyboards can now project an image of a keyboard onto any flat surface allowing you to type almost anywhere. See if you can guess which portion of this book was typed in the back of a bus. I listened to a speech from a technology expert the other day and the changes we are in for this kind of area are absolutely staggering. While I am still failing to get to grips with MP3s, he predicted that by 2010, we will be able to buy a device half the size of the iPod Nano, with every single piece of music ever recorded already loaded onto it. And we will be able to update it in a moment every week if we so wish.

Fear not, however. With all these developments help is at hand in the form of the ubiquitous instruction manual. Every device has one, though too many are of a sort that makes advanced calculus seem like Enid Blyton and hardly help.

It may well be worth persevering, therefore, to perfect your typing skills. There are some documents you may want to originate privately, without the help of a secretary or the entire typing pool seeing and discussing them. Certainly today, whilst typing at a decent speed remains a minority skill, there is still some kudos to be had from just being seen to be doing it well. And for older readers, remember that there is a whole generation coming up behind the older hands who take to all electronic wizardry rather too easily for comfort. It may be politic to keep ahead.

Megalomania Case No 5: *A small point, but a point nevertheless*

MEMORANDUM

TO: All Senior Managers.   1st July
FROM: A.T. Cer, Training Manager.
SUBJECT: Management Training

The Board have asked me to conduct a special one-day seminar on the subject of delegation. This will be held on 19 August in the Board Room, and will be scheduled from 9 am until 5.30 pm. *All* senior managers and heads of department are asked to make sure they attend; this is an important event.

MEMORANDUM

TO: A.T. Cher
FROM: N.O. Waye

Please note the following with regard to your memo of 1st July about the Delegation session to be held in August.

I shall not be attending, but I will send my Assistant.

<u>Moral</u>: If you can score a small point—and do so with something of a flourish once in a while—why not?

Another recipient of this memo left it to their Assistant to compose a reply saying their Manager could not attend.

Very important STOP

There are other different ways of passing a message. Some are now no more like the runner with the message in the forked stick but have modern counterparts in the murderously fast courier bikes, which roar around our cities with a higher accident rate than the Roman chariot. Some communication methods never caught on in business, like the carrier pigeon which will really not accommodate A-4 sized paper and, in any case, cannot be used when birds of prey are about (the normal situation in most organisations). Others are up to date and their technology adds genuinely new elements to the communication process.

Go a few years back. Way back then, telex looked urgent. It had elements passed on by the old-style telegram—an even older system still sadly missed by some people. It was therefore useful, not only when urgency is wanted. The messages contained in them might have been stalled, prevaricated or said nothing at all. By its very nature, however, it shouted, "This is being dealt with urgently!" On the other hand, most people, perhaps conscious of the cost—telex cost per line, the legacy of the telegram— adopted a breathlessly abbreviated style, which is not always compatible with clear comprehension. The story of the message about Cary Grant related earlier makes a strong point against too much abbreviation. If this does happen, then speed and economy are lost as additional messages are passed to and fro to clarify matters.

Similar comments might be made about fax and there are just enough fax machines still around to allow some people to feel that bundles of faxes, preferably heavily annotated and better still, hung on a hook on the wall—in full view—make every workstation or office look more important. More so, of course, if some are clearly from overseas. They highlight Hong Kong and Honolulu with a florescent pen for maximum effect.

Fax is rapidly going the way of the telex, of course, but the e-mail we all now could not do without is still a comparatively recent innovation. Only 10 years or so ago, it did not exist. Earlier on—for a moment—it was something the meaner office managers insisted we could do without. Now, it is almost as universal as the telephone. Soon, we are told, it will not only be available in the office, home and car, and as an integral part of the current generation of mobile phones, but also, in all likelihood, inescapably projected on the insides of our eyeballs. It has the same benefit of speed as the fax, but you are not restricted on length and can send messages using a variety of layouts (though most e-mails do not win prizes for graphic excellence—maybe you can make yours an exception).

One interesting thing that has happened with e-mail is that people who would normally insist on sending all external messages as perfect formal letters, send informal memo-style e-mails to the same people. There is, as yet, apparently no set form on this, which means you can inject more or less formality into your message without looking inefficient or over friendly, though the biggest hazard is probably to be too informal and either fail to communicate clearly or offend.

Like faxes once did, e-mails speak of an urgency and importance which can be useful. What we have lost is the fact that the shiny paper most fax machines used allowed messages to fade away to invisibility after some time. This could be useful to the office politician—a memorandum with a built in self-destruct mechanism, allowing you to say, "You will find it in my fax of..." with real confidence that, in due course, they will not—provided you do not underestimate the fade-out time. Anyway, e-mail is here to stay for the moment and the delete button works in a split second. Actually, given my level of technological knowledge, that is probably a millisecond or some such. Incidentally, for the technically minded, a split second can be defined as the length of time it takes in a busy street between the traffic light in front of you turning from red to green, and the driver of the car behind sounding his or her horn.

Not all communication is in writing of course. Much is done verbally in meetings (which is reviewed in the next chapter), whether face to face or taking place in a more formal setting which has its own problems and opportunities.

Now, do it standing up

This heading is not a reference to those ubiquitous double entendre mottoes and bumper stickers, such as 'Craftsmen make it last longer' and 'Windsurfers do it standing up!' (and clowns, presumably, falling down) but to the skill of making an effective formal presentation. This is one of those sheep-and-goats factors that really do sort the men from the boys. What is more, it is one which is increasingly important in an ever-wider range of organisational jobs. It is a skill with which you can automatically project confidence, credibility, capability and clout; and sometimes do so to a degree way beyond reality. It is no good being able to lay out a plan of action to a colleague across the desk in the office in an rresistibly persuasive way if, when you are asked to present it to the Board—"... just 10 minutes or so and a few slides, you know ..."—you are reduced to an inarticulate heap of jelly and do not do justice to the thing at all.

Yet doing a presentation is not necessarily so easy. As the saying goes, 'The human brain is a wonderful thing, it starts working the moment you are born and keeps on working right up to the moment you stand up to speak in public'. Presenting is, in fact, a skill like any other. As such it can be learnt. Virtually, everyone can, if not become a great orator, at least become a competent presenter. The many who have attended presentation skills development courses are witness to this fact.

> **66** A speaker who does not strike oil in ten minutes should stop boring. **99**
>
> *Louis Nizer*

It is by no means everyone's stock in trade. The following few paragraphs, adapted from my book *How to craft successful business presentations* (Foulsham Publishing), make the problems—and some of the political implications—clear.

"We all have to do lots of things we do not like. Some are just distasteful things like unblocking the sink or cleaning someone else's ring off the bath; others are worse—things we feel seriously ill equipped to do well."

Take speaking: we can all have a chat, swap gossip or say, "What time do you call this?" to the postman, but sometimes we may have to do something rather more formal. But ask many people to stand up and address an audience and they go to pieces, or to Reykjavik —anything at all rather than do it.

It can be done, however. Anyone can make an acceptable, workman-like speech and many find that it is something at which they can excel if they go about it the right way. Few people are natural public speakers; and those that make it look easy tend to do so because they work at it.

But stand up totally unprepared and, oh dear, things can go wrong. People stumble, hesitate and sweat. They begin every other sentence with the superfluous word 'Basically'. Asked to comment on some project, they say, "Um, er … at this moment in time we are making considerable progress with the necessary preliminary work prior to the establishment of the initial first phase of work," when they mean, "We aim to start soon".

Just when they should be impressing their audience with their expertise and confidence, and making them interested in what they have to say, they upset or confuse them. Exactly what is said and how it is put matters; indeed, there may be a great deal hanging on it. As Bob Hope used to say of his early performances, "If the audience liked you, they didn't applaud, they let you live."

At worst, people go on too long so that their explanations explain nothing and where they are going or leading to is wholly unclear. Some fidget endlessly, others remain stock still, gripping the table or lectern in front of them until their knuckles go white and fear rises from them like a mist. Still, others are apt to pick holes in people in the audience, or their noses. If they use slides, then they can only be read from the back of the room with a telescope. This fact is made worse by their asking brightly, "Can you see alright at the back?" despite the fact that there is precious little they can do about it if the answer is "No", and in any case they should not be asking, they should know their slides are legible. They barely pause for breath, as they rush from one word to the next, many of which are inappropriately chosen and as many more too long. Indeed, the only long word which some speakers appear ignorant of is 'rehearsal'.

Of course, a lucky few believe that making a speech or doing a presentation is second nature to them. They know they can wing it. They are convinced that they know their stuff and how to put it over. The first rule then for the inappropriately overconfident is, to assume that the audience is as thick as they look and will, provided the right level of impenetrable gobbledegook is hit, instantly conclude that they are in the presence of a master.

'Winging it' means that if they want people to actually understand even the gist of what is said, then some care must be taken. So, they talk v-e-r-y s-l-o-w-l-y, use simple words and generally proceed on the basis that the audience have the brains of retarded dormice. They spell out complicated bits in CAPITAL LETTERS, speaking MORE LOUDLY as they do so. Though they are always careful not to be condescending, as that will upset people (you do know what 'condescending' means don't you?).

For this kind of speakers, being on their feet is something to savour. They need only the briefest of introductions and they are away. Moving quickly past the first slide without noticing that it is upside down, the coins in their trouser pocket rattling at 90 decibels and the audience hanging on their every repetitive mannerism they mutter to themselves, "If he scratches his backside whilst standing on one leg again, I'm walking out." It makes lesser mortals feel all too sadly inadequate—even the famous: it was Mark Twain who reportedly said, "It normally takes me three weeks to prepare a good impromptu speech." Poor man. Just as well, he was a good writer.

But even speakers convinced of their own abilities, however wrongly they hold that view, should not hog all the opportunities for themselves just because such opportunities are fun. They should give others a chance. Next time someone says, "Will you give the presentation?" they may hand over the task to whoever displays the least enthusiasm (maybe to you?). It will do them good they think; and they may feel that there is nothing quite like inflicting sheer terror on a friend or colleague to make them feel superior. If you can present well, here is a classic political opportunity.

❝ Speeches are like babies, easy to conceive—but hard to deliver. **❞**

Pat O'Malley

Putting someone in front of an important audience knowing that they would rather chew off their own fingers than sit and listen to someone who cannot make the simplest point clear, is rather like pushing the speaker into a lion's den. Without an understanding of how to go about it in the right way, he will be in deep, deep trouble. No audience will warm to a speaker who is ill prepared and who flounders through a speech that is tedious, confusing and poorly delivered. And nor will the speaker—though poor, unthinkingly believes that he can—'wing it'. Furthermore, no poor speaker is likely to magically acquire the requisite skills instantaneously in the few seconds between being introduced and rising to his feet to speak.

So if you are not, in fact, a natural—and few people are—you need to give it some thought before you get to your feet; once you are actually in the lion's den it is a little late to discover that salvation is not guaranteed by saying, "Nice pussycat."

If you know *how* to present, the importance of preparation, your audience, how to get off to a good start, how to structure and pace what you say, how to lay the emphasis where you intend it to be, you will finish on a high note. If you look the audience in the eye, are physically articulate—use gestures appropriately—look and sound confident, know how to field questions, find the right example, illustration, story or humorous aside and use visual aids in the right way, you will do it better. And if you can do it well, it becomes a powerful tool in your political armoury. There is an old saying that goes 'If it is in black and white it must be true'. The same principle applies to presentations as to things in print. If a presentation is well crafted then that fact boosts the credibility of its content. And vice versa— *What a rotten presentation, I bet the ideas were rubbish too.*

A good presentation can enthuse or convince, where a poor one would not. A well made point or carefully phrased question can prompt discussion that will lead a group towards your way of thinking. A clear explanation— (perhaps augmented by a good slide) may get people's understanding of a difficult point, or making a more sensible and prompt decision as a result.

Plans, budget, ideas, careers may all stand or fall based on the quality of presentation. People are influenced by style and approach—it can carry them along, lay down the law, or get attention or consideration where a less inspired approach will not. They are also influenced by detail; one good slide, perhaps a graph, and people are saying, "I hadn't seen it that way before." And by precision: do not say, "... if we get down to this immediately we can have everything sorted out fast." If you leave people to make inferences from something vague, they will almost certainly get it wrong. In this case, sooner rather than later. So, if you mean "... if we phase this in three stages over the next two months, we should see a five per cent change by the end of the quarter," say so.

The poor presentation is full of such phrases as "... err,

um, right, basically what I want to say is actually ..." (all the worst presentations have the word 'basically' in the first few moments—usually the first word of a sentence.); "... sorry, this slide is rather unclear, but what it should show is ..." (*why* is unclear?), "I have rather overrun my time ..." (always finish on time); and "Now, when I said earlier there are three key reasons for this proposal, I should have said four, because I forgot to mention ..." (structure is vital). Any such tendency can leave one in a good case struggling, and a weaker one stone dead. On the other hand it is perfectly possible for a poor case, which is well presented, to win out over a better one, which is poorly presented. Good presentation skills can add authority, certainty, accuracy, urgency and so on, far beyond what the core message actually contains. There may well be some occasions when you need all the elements of a first class presentation to be sure of getting your case over.

There are limits, of course. The content of the presentation needs some substance. You cannot make bricks without straw. However, there are those who, with only a few stalks but with some conviction and skills in presenting, can build a really respectable wall.

You must therefore never be at a loss for a few appropriate words (if not appropriate, then appropriated will do). Presentation is a vital skill; no self-respecting office politician can afford to be without it.

> ❝I like the way you always manage to state the obvious with a sense of real discovery.❞
>
> *Gore Vidal*

Now here's a vine thing

Every organisation, large or small, has a 'grapevine'. Nearly always, it is hated and resented by the management. Often, the management attempts to clamp down on it. Usually its attempts to do so are to no avail. The 'grapevine' can take many forms: from a labyrinthine network with tentacles in every corner of the office, to one—dedicated—person. In some companies 80 per cent of the 'grapevine' is one person. Perhaps it is the tea lady. When I first joined a consulting firm, we had one (appropriately called Mrs Brewer) who moved constantly around the company, listening to everything, and passing on much of it. Thus, most people in the company could, by mid afternoon, know a comment picked up with the 11 o'clock tea delivery. When this happens, whether a comment remains in the same form or not, of course, is another matter. If the original comment was exaggerated, unclear or if it has been too long on the 'circuit', it may become difficult, or even impossible, to comprehend accurately. In Britain there was an old wartime example of the message, "Send reinforcements we are going to advance" being passed down the line until it became "Send 3s 4d[1] we are going to a dance." This process may distort the truth unrecognisably—assuming it was the truth in the first place—though sometimes the truth is still lurking within for those sufficiently adept at reading between the lines.

The 'grapevine' will tell you a variety of things, all different in nature. Some things are just tittle-tattle—"… and you know that Mary is leaving, not before time either,

---

[1] Old style British non-decimal currency of shillings and pence within the pound.

nothing fits her any more ..." —though it may be of some use in itself, or provide early warning of something more important. Some are factual—"John's going to the States for a month"—catch him quickly for that decision you want before he goes. Some are only rumours—"I was told by Jane that she had heard from ..." One thing leads to another. Rumour has it that there is trouble in the Dispatch department. It seems that someone in dispatch has been fired. We hear a strike is on the cards. Then suddenly it is proven correct, and nothing moves out of the building for several weeks. At which point, as all these progress, is it worth making sure that *your* key packages are off the premises and en route to their destination as you anticipate the trouble pending? Pick the right moment to act and you will stay ahead of the game. There is one key thing above all that you must remember about the 'grapevine'.

You must use it.

The 'grapevine' will always be there. Listen. Listen carefully and be prepared to interpret. Feed things in, but with care. Choose your moment, and the point of input. Keep in touch with various points around the network of contacts and individuals that the 'grapevine' connects. This may be time-consuming and detract you from other activities but it is important and potentially, you may have much to gain from doing so. But, and it is an important but, do not be seen as a blatant 'grapeviner' as this will often be read by others as at best negative, and at worst subversive. It is a fine line to tread perhaps between being well informed through the informal network, and being marked down as a disruptive rumourmonger.

> 66 It has always been desirable to tell the truth, but seldom if ever necessary. 99
>
> *A.J. Balfour*

Not only is the 'grapevine' a useful device to secure or pass on information about a host of small things; it can have altogether more substantial results.

Hype, hype-hurrah!

'Hype' is now an ubiquitous word for an intensive 'splurge' of publicity. Applied most readily to pop records and new movies (especially the kind of movie with II, III, or IV after the title) it also applies to causes or ideas. Bob Geldolf has used 'hype' to rally support for disadvantaged people in Africa; but the same can apply on a much more local scale within the office.

Apparently unprompted, certain ideas suddenly seem to become widely known and widely supported, yet no one quite knows why this is so or what caused this to happen. The campaign somehow acquired a momentum of its own and often the starting point remains obscure. Except, of course, to whoever sowed the seeds in the first place. They know. It starts with a whisper, made in the right quarter. Surely, it would be a good idea to ... get a new photocopier, move offices, increase a particular budget, get rid of such and such a department or person. Then it becomes more strident. Everybody agrees that ... We must ... And so on. Who gets told something first is important. They must be interested in the outcome, and thus be likely to repeat and discuss the matter—even to embellish it.

In a large organisation several seeds may need to be sown. In different parts of the office several nudges may be necessary to keep the process moving: nothing too obvious, of course, if you do not want to be seen to be in the vanguard of the campaign. There is nothing like being able to raise an issue, or see it raised, with a good groundswell of support. Too little and the powers that be do not notice; too much and it may be rejected on principle because it smacks of blackmail. The secret is in the timing. Pick the right moment to sow the seeds or punch home an attack and another small objective may be achieved.

This is the ultimate use of the 'grapevine'. It can constitute grand scale deception and propaganda, and can be a very powerful influence, changing views around the organisation in a persuasive way.

Have I got you where you want me

We cannot leave the subject of communication without having a word about one aspect of it with which some skill is virtually mandatory for the office politician: negotiation.

❝ If you want a hamster, you start by asking for a pony. **❞**

Posting on the internet by Annabel, age 6

Wonderful! The youngster quoted above apparently has some inherent knowledge or insight into the process of negotiation. It may stand her in good stead later in life because negotiation—bargaining to put it simply—is used in so many different contexts.

Negotiation, the process of making a deal and agreeing with the terms on which it is arranged, is an important and ubiquitous business skill. It is essentially an interactive communication skill and one very much linked to being persuasive.

Good negotiators are in a strong position to make a good impression and a good deal. Much can be riding on the outcome of a negotiation. Success can make money, save time or secure your future (and your reputation). To negotiate and do so successfully is to deploy a technique that can work positively for you in a host of different ways. The overall deal you strike may be vital, and individual elements of it can be significant—perhaps very significant. For example, without a little negotiation regarding the delivery date for the manuscript of this work, I could not have taken on writing it and would have missed the opportunity that writing it provides for me (and, I hope, for you).

The techniques of negotiation are many and varied. It needs the right approach, the right attitude and attention to a multitude of details on the way through. Like so many business skills it cannot be applied by rote, its use must be tailored—intelligently tailored—to the individual circumstances on a case by case basis. It has elements of being an adversarial process about it and thus, needs handling with care. Individual techniques may be common sense in some ways but they do need deploying with some sensitivity. You can as easily find that someone is running rings around you as that you are tying up the deal of a lifetime.

66 There are two fools in every market place. One asks to little, the other asks too much. 99

Traditional Russian proverb

Negotiation is best defined thus: Communication is the basic process, the flow of information between people that informs, instructs and more. More important here is persuasive communication. This is designed to produce agreement and action in another person. As such, this may have a wealth of applications including selling where the agreement is to buy something.

When persuasion has worked and agreement is there, at least in principle, negotiation may then take over. It is concerned with the relationship between two parties where the needs of both are largely in balance. It is the process of bargaining that arranges the basis on which an agreement will be concluded—the terms and conditions under which the deal will be struck.

Consider a simple example. In the classic case of wage bargaining, the employer and employees want to reach an agreement (for the employer—to secure the workforce and keep the business running; for the employees—so that the process of negotiating is over, and they can get on with earning at a new, improved, rate). This process of balance defines the process. In persuasion, the first stage is to get agreement—from the point of view of the seller, to get what he or she wants—but beyond that, negotiation is what decides the 'best deal'. Thus, if you are buying a car, the things that need arrangement are all those making up the 'package' which goes beyond just the car itself. Such factors may include: the finance, discounts, non-standard extras to be included with the car (leather seats, perhaps), delivery, trade in of an existing vehicle and so on. It is not a good deal to get a low price but fail to get anything else you want and drive away in a Skoda. (Sorry Skoda, I know you make great cars these days, but it is just traditional).

66 I always win. You always lose. What could be fairer than that? **99**

Ashleigh Brilliant

Negotiation is characterised by various factors:

- *An interactive and balanced process*
  It is an interactive and balanced process and one where the outcome must, by definition, be agreeable to both parties (though that does not mean both parties will necessarily regard the outcome as ideal). This is usually referred to as the 'win-win' factor. The office politician will probably prefer win—WIN.

- *An adversarial element is inherent within the process as each party vies to get the best deal that they can*

This aspect must be kept in check. If it gets out of hand negotiations may deteriorate into a slanging match with both parties making demands to which neither will ever agree so that the whole process is stillborn. And you will want a result.

- *'Trading'*
  A major part of the process of bargaining is one of what is called 'trading'. In other words, as the terms and conditions are discussed—the variables as they are called—they must be traded to create a balance on an 'If I agree to this, you will need to let me have that' basis.

- *Give and take*
  A fair amount of give and take is necessary, and the 'to and fro' discussion takes time; negotiation cannot be rushed.

- *A ritual element is involved*
  Negotiation must be seen to be doing justice to the task it addresses. Time is one element of this.

Simply put, the process of negotiation involves juggling the three key factors—information, time and power. Consider these in turn:

- *Information*
  The old saying that information is power is certainly true in negotiation. Both parties want to know, as much

as possible, about the other—the person (or people), their needs, priorities, intention and approach. A better understanding on one side or the other allows a more accurate deployment of the skills and gives that side an incontrovertible advantage. It is a mistake to assume that your adversary is an unmitigated peasant—you need to understand him, her or them.

- *Time*

  Always, pressure and urgency and specific deadlines may be imposed on any situation, often coming from outside the control of the person negotiating. For example, someone's boss may be imposing tight timing (for reasons explained or unexplained). Similarly, circumstances may affect timing, for example in the way the publication of a company's annual accounts— announcing record results—might make concluding a pay deal ahead of the announcement a priority for management. On the other hand, time and timing is one of the raw materials of most negotiations and it is said, with some truth, that there has not been a deadline in history that was not negotiable—so never assume one you are offered is fixed.

❝ When a man tells me he is going to put all his cards on the table, I always look up his sleeve. **❞**

Lord Hore-Belisha

- *Power*

  Many factors can add weight—power—to your ability to negotiate. The phrase 'having someone over a barrel' picks up this point. It means power is very much on one side. Power stems form two main areas. The *power of precedent* is the equivalent of the 'self-fulfilling prophecy'—we know something cannot be done because a certain past experience tells us so. The result? We avoid even raising an issue and the power moves to the other side. Negotiation demands an open mind, a thorough search for everything that might assist—taking a chance or a risk is part of the process and doing so and addressing every possibility regardless of precedent gives power and improves the chances of success.

  The other kind is the *power of legitimacy*: this is power projected by authority. Peoples' attitude to what can be negotiated comes, in part, from where and how they see something originates. For example, even something as simple as a form or a notice is often taken as a gospel. Checking in into a hotel, how many people do other than fill in the complete registration form? Very few. Most take it as a given that it must be done, yet in my experience, if you ask, then often, a few key details are sufficient. The point here is that the authority may be real or it may be assumed or implied. In other words, power is intentionally invested in something to apparently give it more power and make it weigh more heavily in the balance. This may be very minor. Someone says, "That would be against policy"—and suddenly someone else feels less able to challenge the point. Even when both parties understand this principle it still adds an additional element to discussions who, all the time, must assess the real power being brought to the table as the meeting proceeds.

So negotiation demands that proposals are made and discussed. In the simple example above, negotiation can fail not because it is done badly but because it is avoided and not done at all. The situation is then likely to turn acrimonious and argument is all that ensues.

At the end of the day all the parties involved need to understand the nature of negotiation. It may be adversarial, but we are aiming at a mutually agreeable outcome—what is usually referred to as a 'win-win' outcome. If one party goes headlong for the best deal regardlessly, the likelihood is that they will push the other into a corner and that they will feel unable to agree to anything; the negotiation stalls. If both parties accept that some compromise is necessary, then the outcome is likely to be better for both. Thus, negotiation is about seeking common ground, relating to the other people and their concerns, participating in 'to and fro' debate, but not insisting on a totally rigid agenda. It means asking questions and listening to the answers, disclosing (some) information, openly stating a point of view, building a relationship and treating the other person with respect.

Negotiation, throughout, must aim at agreement and actively act to avoid a stalemate. If persuasion answers the question: Will this person agree?—then negotiation must address the question: On what basis will this person agree? Forgive me, we are getting too serious, but this is a vital technique and it also makes the point that with anything in communication you must operate with some skill. These are not matters which you can just hope just to 'wing it' (despite Annabel's apparent instincts!). Some study may be necessary here—see 'Read on' towards the end of the book.

66 The fellow who agrees with everything you say is either a fool, or he is getting ready to skin you. 99

Frank McKinney Hubbard

Key guidelines to success

- *Always tell the truth.* You cannot be given 9 out of 10 for honesty. But there are doubtless occasions when you should not tell the whole story.
- *Do not broadcast your successes.* People will resent it, and that becomes self-defeating. Be satisfied with having got what you want and resist the temptation to crow about it too much. If you do so in the wrong way then it will definitely get people's backs up. There is a balance to be struck here.
- *Stay close.* There is no doubt that there are those people who can wage a campaign from the darkest corners

of the organisation's empire. This is true whether that office is in far away Auckland (remembering the press is once said to have reported of New Zealand: "Terrible tragedy; two and a half million people marooned in Pacific") or a sub-basement of a small regional branch office—but most find communication easiest within reach of the corridors of power.

- *Learn to be a good communicator.* And it does need to be learnt. It will then make up for a few other failings or unfavourable circumstances.

- *Be brief.* People have a short attention span. Keep memos, reports, presentations, explanations or requests brief. Watch, particularly, when things must be in writing. One page may be all you need (yes this is page 94 of this book, but would you have bought a book that was only one page long?) Business paperwork is the bane of most people's lives; everyone will love you if you do not add to their burden. Though remember, sometimes the old maxim about the best place to hide a tree being in a forest may be good advice. I now notice that this is the longest item in this summary; but it is an important point. Additionally it … Enough!

- *A case is often best presented as a range of options.* A range with one that somehow meets the need very much better than the others.

05

Management and Meetings

> 66 Meetings are indispensable when you don't want to do anything. 99
>
> *J.K. Galbraith*

Management matters

If management is the art of getting things done through other people, rather than doing it for them (which it is), then maybe office politics can be described as the art of getting things done by manipulating people. Not that manipulating is the right word for your own entirely constructive attempts to get your own way, of course. There can be little doubt, however, that politics is a little easier if you are at management level and have a few of your own people to involve in the fray. Many of the processes of management, in fact, have about them the opportunity for a little political manoeuvring and can have side effects beyond their more obvious intent. Managers have to recruit, organise, develop, motivate and control the people who report to them. They have to make sure these people perform, achieving necessary and targeted results, or they are both in trouble. But along the way, there are broader implications that must be considered other than just achieving the plan, budget or whatever other objectives have been set.

Imagine you are a manager for a moment (you may be one already or aim to be) and consider some of these management processes in turn:

Recruitment, the process of adding or replacing members of your team, is clearly very important. The success of your people will reflect on you; so too will any of their failures. It is therefore worth taking time and trouble to find the right people for any vacancy. Yet the business world is full of managers who seem to think recruitment is easy. Wrong. Very wrong: it is one of the most difficult things to get right, and an unsystematic approach can make failure that much more likely.

Managers are rarely able to recognise the right person, by instinct, as they walk through the door. They often rely too much on hunch, formula or any sort of white magic, which might shortcut the grizzly process of interviewing and assessing people. As a result, they recruit English graduates on the assumption that they can spell, but not add up; secretaries and typists who say they can type 70 words per minute so confidently that they are not tested and subsequently prove unable to recognise 'a' from 'b'. And they select accountants who do not know how to read a balance sheet. Having said that, there is a story told of the manager recruiting a new accountant who asked each applicant "What is 2+2?" All the applicants said "4", except the last who on replying, "What do you want it to be?" was promptly hired. One of the other applicants admitted to taking three attempts to pass his final accountancy exams although the official record showed it was four!

The big question about recruitment for the office politician is whether likely candidates are potential allies or possible rivals. Some managers want all their subordinates to be 'Yes-men', and remind one of the manager who said to the applicant, "I think you have the right qualifications for the job: you have the makings of a first underling." Others want their recruits to think, operate and even appear just like themselves. This practice is known as 'mirror recruitment'—bosses or managers filling their department with seeming clones of themselves. You, no doubt, want to work for someone who gives you responsibility and support where necessary; who is consistent, and from whom you learn something; who makes you think and where the relationship—working together—makes you and the business stronger. So too, of course, do those people who work for you. It makes best sense to seek out people who can do a first class job and whose success will contribute to the smooth running of your department. For everyone whose position is usurped by a member of their own staff, there are 10 who run into trouble because the inadequate performance of a subordinate is seen by others, especially the more senior, as a sign of their incompetence.

So hire the good people, give them their head, let them get on with it, but watch your back while they do so.

Organisation of those working with you is important also. Without clear roles and responsibilities, those around you will never contribute as much as they should. Job descriptions and challenging objectives do not only ensure that their achievements will be on plan, but will reflect well on you when they are achieved. If your staff are busy, they will have little time for politicking of their own. Indeed, if they are successful and happy, they will be less inclined to indulge in office politics. Delegation, on the other hand, gives you more time. Whilst a fear of a subordinate doing something better than the manager—rather than fear that he or she will fail—is classically a prime reason things often do not get delegated, those who successfully rise up in an organisation are usually good at delegating. They would never have gotten so much done and made such a mark if they had tried to do everything themselves. As an example, the best manager I have ever had was a superlative delegator. So too for you—delegate and enhance your success.

Developing people is one of the first principles of successful management. There is a saying that, 'if you can't train, you can't manage'. There is a great deal of truth to it. If you wholeheartedly pitch yourself into not just supporting but developing your people, however, will you win friends and influence people or create a monster that will take over your job?

The advantages normally outweigh the risks. You need an effective team, and helping your people do a better job is something they find motivational. Those you help in this way may regard themselves as in your debt. An expanding range of talent and capabilities within the section creates a resource that can be useful in all sorts of ways over time. It increases the capacity of the group to take on new things, and a reputation for this sort of innovation is not a bad one to have. You are not, in fact, paid to have all the good ideas, but you are paid to make sure that there are enough of them to achieve the end result.

The answer to the resentful manager who whines, "What happens if I train my people and the investment is wasted because they leave?" is simply another question: "What happens if you don't train them and they stay?"

Motivating people is as important as developing them. It is not a bit of good having a team of people who are able to do what you want but where none of them have any real inclination to do so. Motivation is rather like sex—you want to practice it—but it is best not to talk too much about it. In other words, the prudent manager will make sure that he has a well-motivated team. Indeed, it is worth being seen by your colleagues to have such a team—but they should wonder why it is that your team is so well motivated as well as puzzled over how you apparently achieve this so effortlessly. This is not so easy to achieve as it may seem. Motivation does not just happen. Creating a positive motivational feeling amongst a group of people takes time, consideration and, if the 'motivational climate' is to be kept just right, involves systematic, ongoing action—rather, as the temperature of a glass house for plants can be kept steady in a number of ways —turning the heat up, opening or closing the windows, raising or lowering the blinds. So whether people are well motivated or not is the end result of a combination of many different actions. These may vary from the manager recognising an individual's achievement with a "Well done" (Do you work for someone who does that as often as they should? Do you do it sufficiently often for your subordinates?) through to elaborate incentive schemes.

Overheard:

! "In this company motivation is all carrot and stick—with no carrot."

The trick is to work invisibly yet carefully and regularly at this so that your immediate colleagues think the sun shines out of your every orifice, and others are put at a disadvantage by the positive attitude of those around you.

Ten ways to keep subordinates in their place (but inhibit performance)

- Make them responsible for too much or too little.
- Do not define their responsibilities.
- Set unreasonable targets (and refuse to discuss them).
- Assume everything is their fault.
- Criticise everything they do (preferably in public).
- Do not delegate, do the job (or at least the interesting tasks) for them.
- Keep checking up on them (especially when they do

not expect it, and when whatever they are doing is still
half finished).

- Talk about them behind their backs.
- Let them pass on any bad news (whilst you pass on
  the good).
- If ever they do well, do not acknowledge the fact,
  either to them or to others.

Control must be exercised. It is, in fact, much more difficult
to thrive as a *laissez-faire* manager than as one who runs an
unashamedly tight ship. People tend to not respect you if
you are draconian, but will do so still, but less, if you let all
and sundry get away with murder. The key thing is to be
consistent. People must know where they are with you, know
what you stand no nonsense about and what standards you
set. It is not necessary to be democratic (indeed trying to
be so can be a nightmare of ineffectiveness—the office was
never any place for democracy). It is not even necessary to
be fair about everything as long as you are seen to be equally
unfair to all and reasons are explained. Remember too that
just saying, "Because I say so," palls extremely quickly and
will likely make people rambunctious.

How you are thought of in terms of your management
capabilities and style (and what you achieve with them) is
going to contribute to your overall image in a major way.
Some managers manage. They are seen as people to be
respected; as people for whom others will move mountains
for—large mountains that is. (There is an Icelandic proverb
that says, "Mediocrity is climbing molehills without

sweating.") Other managers are better compared with the gardener in a cemetery—there are lots of people under them, but none of them is taking much notice.

In fact, there are many grades of management ability though one may perhaps divide them into four groups. It is said that there are managers who:

- do not know what is happening
- talk about what is happening
- watch what is happening
- make things happen

Some may get by, some may rise to be chief assistant to the assistant chief, but only those in the fourth group stand the best chance of getting to the top. This is even more the case if they are not only good at working with other people, but can also judge these people's value, worth, attitude and how their own behaviour is likely to effect them.

Overheard:

 "One thing you can say about my manager, his indecision is final."

How do you assess others? Are you good at judging people? Of course you are. Certainly, I doubt very much, however, that you are about to admit otherwise. Finding someone who does is like discovering a man who will confess to being a bad driver, or a woman who will tell you she has enough shoes (Excuse me while I check. "Sue, do you have ..."—no, not a good idea). On the other hand, your assessment of others is very important to you. It follows that it may be better to admit, to yourself at least, any uncertainty about those around you. Is George really harmless? Does John actually present any threat? Or are the quiet ones the ones to watch? Are those with the low profiles really second division or just biding their time? You may not be able to insist that all your colleagues take a psychometric test, but you can certainly refuse to take their outward personae at face value. 'Better safe than sorry,' as the saying goes. Always bear in mind how the face presented to the world may disguise a person's real intentions and take a second look. Better still, a regular and long look.

Your face may need attention also. Check.

A group of people at least, say within one department, have broadly the same goals but even then, managing them successfully is not always without its problems. There are, however, other groupings and combinations—in which people come together in the organisation—which present altogether greater and more difficult problems.

One to one, and a few more

There is a management training film titled *Meetings, Bloody Meetings* (produced by Video Arts and well worth a look). Whether the film company coined the phrase or not (probably not), the company's using it has turned the phrase into a popular cliché. Is not that exactly how many of us think of meetings—or at least about many of them? But meetings are here to stay—to be endured, to be participated in or to be taken advantage of by the office politician.

> 66 Meetings are rather like cocktail parties. You don't want to go, but you are cross not to be asked. 99
>
> *Jilly Cooper*

Hell has been described as one long meeting—one that has no agenda, never reaches any conclusion and to which there is no end. We all know the kind of meeting we dread most. It is called at short notice. It is described as being 'urgent' or 'most important'—or as both. Because there is no clear notice of the meeting, there is confusion about where it is to be held. The conference room is already booked, and what is more, another meeting is already under way inside. So, possession being nine points of the law, the group is forced to repair to an empty office. That proves to be a size too small. One result of all these is that the meeting starts late. One member of the group is unaccounted for, and he is expected to take the minutes. A (reluctant) volunteer is found for this chore and the meeting finally gets under way. Within 10 minutes the air is thick with smoke, within 15 the chairs are uncomfortable, within 20 it is clear that the agenda is being made up as the meeting proceeds and that finishing by lunchtime is not on it. There is no coffee or tea and—bored out of your mind—you note that there are 376 triangular designs on the wallpaper and that Chris could do with cutting his hair, especially in his ears and nose.

The first item is pondered for an hour and a half and no conclusion is reached. Everyone disagrees. Certain people take umbrage and one leaves the meeting having discovered, after all this time, that they are in the wrong room. Finally, a decision is made. It is decided —unanimously too—to defer the item to another meeting. Not just another meeting in fact, but to devolve the matter to a specially convened committee. Will you be on it? At this stage, if not before, you pray that you will wake up and find it is all a bad dream.

There are two kinds of meetings: yours, which means you have to chair them; and those convened by other people, which you have to attend. The first means you have to do some work, but that you do have a degree of control. The second means you have to do some work if you want to stand any chance of getting your own way, as you have little or no control. The influence you can, in part, bring to bear can be through the kind of things mentioned in the nightmare vision described earlier. The late notice, general chaos, discomfort and so on may have all been contrived for the express purpose of ensuring that no conclusion was reached. After all, more people probably spend more time in meetings trying to delay or stop something from happening, than ever do in arranging that it will. Sometimes as the agendas are laid round the table and the pencils are sharpened, less comforting factors are built in for the express purpose of putting someone who will attend at a disadvantage. Alternatively, influence has to be brought to bear through the actual processes involved in any meeting.

There are five key stages, all with possibilities for the astute politician:

Planning is the first. Meetings do not just happen (unless they are like the one just described). They need to be given some thought beforehand. Why is the meeting being held? Is it just because it has been a month since the last one? This is never a sufficiently good reason. Indeed, you might score some points by banning any meeting held in your organisation from having a period of time in its description—no more weekly this and monthly that. Or is it because there are specific objectives to be achieved? You do not have to be the chairperson to influence this, maybe anyone can set the agenda, or at least make suggestions … or just proposing there actually is an agenda may be a step in the right direction. Items that you want to be focused on should never be allowed to appear under A.O.B.—this stands, of course, for 'Any Other Business'—and sometimes the miscellaneous items listed under this A.O.B. seem to take up 90 per cent of the time of the meeting. Anything you regard as vital should have its own scheduled spot. Conversely, items you do not want much time spent on should always go under A.O.B.; and items you do not want to get to at all should go at the bottom of A.O.B.

Doing your homework is the golden rule. Check the information you will need before and at the meeting. See if any lobbying is appropriate. A quiet word before the meeting can substitute for many an angry one at it. Consider what papers need circulating ahead of the meeting and whether they will be read even if they are indeed, circulated. Someone also has to consider the physical things about any meeting. Where will it be held? Will it be better for you if it is in your office, on your territory, or on neutral ground? Who should attend? And of course, often far more important, who should not attend? The main purpose of some meetings is not to discuss whatever the topic of the meeting is, but to make those not attending feel left out. There may be a host of other issues to think about as a meeting is set up, yes, one very important one is time. When will the meeting be set to take place? Certain times are advantageous to a number of people, some to others. If you are an early morning person, then you may do well to start your meetings at 8 am. If you live round the corner from the office, then an afternoon meeting at 5.15—just when some of the others are worrying about their journey home and the vagaries of the transport or traffic situation—may suit nicely. At least, a meeting so scheduled will not run on. Indeed, there is a definite case for any meeting to have a starting as well as a finishing time. If you do not want a meeting to last forever, then picking a time concluding with a natural break, lunch perhaps, makes sense. Participants weigh continuing discussion in the balance against the pangs of hunger.

66 If a problem causes many meetings, the meetings eventually become more important than the problem. **99**

Arthur Bloch

Pre-notification is the second stage. Quite simply, you should not walk into a meeting without a clear idea of what it is all about—unless you see the meeting as a form of ambush or something that is unknown. You may want to spring something on the people involved in the meeting. Otherwise, send round or ask for a clear agenda and do so sufficiently well in advance for preparation to take place around the group. As was said earlier, this is an opportunity to place items within the meeting where you want them.

Once the event is planned, once you are prepared, then the event itself can take place. A meeting may have a clear purpose, but the underlying intentions of some or all of the participants may do more to dictate what actually happens while it takes place. The meeting may take on a steamroller aspect, an underlying intention to delay may rapidly become apparent, or it may soon be clear that the most important thing is for the meeting to provide an ego trip for one of those present. There is a host of underlying intentions for any meeting. And delay, as has been said, may often be one of them—which makes me wonder if it is worth scheduling a meeting with the publisher to persuade them to move on the deadline for the manuscript of this book? Delay is often intended but it is seldom stated as such. The meeting needs a positive purpose, an impressive statement of intent, something like, "This meeting will consider whether further investigation should be carried out into the project, before a recommendation is made to the main Board concerning the possibility of undertaking a feasibility study." This kind of statement sounds infinitely more impressive than simply saying, "We will talk some more but do nothing yet." If there must be inertia, then for goodness sake, let us at least have some creative inertia. Maybe I could say the dog ate my first draft; sorry, I digress.

Sometimes, however, despite all the traditions of life in an organisation, there is a meeting at which the intention is to decide to actually do something. In this event you need to consider carefully what line you will take. Do you lead the proposal? After all, as Arthur Koestler once said, "If the creator had a purpose in equipping us with a neck, he surely meant us to stick it out." Or are you wiser to bear in mind a saying of William Ridge that goes "When you take the bull by the horns ... what happens is a toss up?" Then again, perhaps you should field three schemes, two—carefully and specifically selected so that they do not quite meet the brief—and designed to be shot down; while one—yours—is successfully carried through. Or you might consider getting someone else to put up the idea, so that he or she gets the flack if others do not immediately approve it—and you can join in on the right side if that is the case. Whatever tactic you adopt, you must have a back-up position—or two (or three)—up your sleeve. There are a thousand and one options in these kinds of situations. It is not necessary to know, or have thought round them all; considering only a good few hundred of them will suffice. But, more particularly, you should perhaps be sure that you have considered a few more than what the other people at the meeting have.

No review of the subject of meetings would be complete

without a word about that very particular sort of meeting … the committee meeting.

Committees normally involve a number of people meeting a number of times—perhaps on a regular basis—to discuss—perhaps even progress—some specific area or topic. There is a considerable folklore about committees. Everyone knows about the committee that set out to design a horse and finished up with a camel. It is said that the best committees have an odd number of members; and that three is too many. It is said that the ideal committee (or is that phrase itself a contradiction in terms?) consists of two people—with one of them absent. Committee meetings are like any other meeting, but less likely to achieve anything. They may only have been convened to delay something anyway. There are professional 'committee people', who seem to delight in the process of talking around and around a topic without coming to any conclusion. Indeed, there are surely many circumstances where, if you talk continuously for sufficiently long, the problem goes away.

Committees add additional hazards of formality to meetings. They are more likely to have not just a chairperson but an array of officers, who inevitably slow things up—and this, as has been said, is exactly what some people want. So think very carefully whenever you are asked to join, and particularly to play any major part in, a committee. Committees are time consuming. They may lead to nowhere. They may end up taking the blame if things go wrong or alternatively, if nothing happens; and you with them. Despite all the tendencies for delay, there may eventually come a moment when somebody senior wants to know what is happening; or more likely why it is that something is not happening. At such a time the best position may be to have resigned from the committee some time previously on the grounds that "...it was clearly—despite my best efforts—going about things the wrong way."

> 66 A decision is what a man makes when he can't get anyone to serve on a committee. 99
> *Fletcher Knebel*

Last, but regrettably not least, there is that aftermath of meetings—**putting things on the record**. The minutes of some meetings are longer than the meetings themselves; and in some cases, about as useful. Of course, one needs a record of some things, of the decisions made—assuming there were any—if not a verbatim account of every moment of discussion. Writing minutes is an art. They are often never referred to again but if they are, it is regularly the case that what is there in black and white is subject to different interpretations. This is true particularly if the issue is, in any sense, a sensitive one. The moral for minute takers (or checkers) is clear. Make sure that what is down there is clear and cannot be easily subjected to a variety of interpretations; unless of course that is what suits you best.

Incidentally, my favourite story about minutes concerns those being circulated by a high-powered government committee. One member felt something was rubbish and marked the circulating copy. Feeling it would be impolite to put, as he wanted, 'Balls!' he put instead the words 'Round objects'. A week later the document crossed his desk again and underneath his comment someone else had written, 'Who is Round, and why does he object?'

When the bureaucratic rain dance of the meeting is past, you can reflect on whether it achieved your purpose. Was a decision made? And was it the one that you wanted? Or was a negative conclusion reached, at least, for the moment. Was it that this was not the 'right time' for action? Was it that whilst action should be taken, the current proposal as to how matters were to be handled needed to be reworked? Was it that solutions were too technical or other difficulties needed to be found and agreed on before proceeding further; or that the proposition—although agreed on—now needed to be referred to a higher authority for their approval (often the case with budgets)? These latter outcomes may equally be what you intended. Whatever your intention, and whether you achieved it or not, you will always learn something new at a meeting. And it may be something that may help you through the next one. This something may be how someone reacts, what his view of some matter is, where he appears to have a blind spot, or just what time to arrive to get the seat by the door.

Throughout the process there are things to bear in mind—going on in the rest of the world outside the meeting—that may help you inside the meeting. In other words, there are meetings that can be interrupted and others that cannot be. Is the interruption more important than the meeting? It often is, but it can still be judged the wrong way round. For example, a customer enquiry may be much more important than the topic of a internal meeting but if the managing director is attending, then many people will not consider interrupting. On other occasions you may need an interruption. There is a kind of meeting you go into saying to your secretary, "If it is not finished in an hour pass in a note saying there is an important telephone call I need to take." This gives you an opportunity to go out, and either not to return, or return after some time if you wish—just as A.O.B. is starting perhaps. In the time you are away from the meeting figures can be checked, other people or files consulted; this is a tactic that can save time (shortcutting hours of discussion in the absence of the information), or save the day—or both.

Like so much else in organisational life, meetings are what you make them. Whatever has gone on, as the talk subsides, the smoke clears and someone appears to collect the dirty cups, there is always the chance that someone has—if not achieved a major victory—inched his or her case or position forward just a little. The question is … Who?

Ten things to do in boring meetings (Other than discuss business)

- Draft a memo suggesting that the number of meetings held is reduced.
- Doodle (something those either side of you will find enigmatic).

- Psychoanalyse your own doodles (are you really that mixed-up?).
- Write the minutes (before the meeting is over?—what kind of politician are you trying to be?).
- Make a phone call (one that others will be unable to resist listening to).
- Sleep (conserving your energy for better things).
- Count the number of times the word 'basically' (or some buzzword endemic to your organisation) is said—to starve off terminal boredom.
- Work something out—studiously—on your calculator (the kind that 'beeps' on every key).
- Complete the writing of your treatise on "The psychology of interpersonal relationships in meetings and how it influences results".

Another tactic, which is frankly rather fun, is to launch a comment about something that has absolutely nothing to do with the meeting, the agenda or the other people present—and see if anyone notices. That way you might be surprised to realise that you get agreement to something that is really important.

66 When in doubt, don't call a meeting. 99
Mark H McCormack

The right rate of strike
In office life, it is not necessary to be right always. There are very few organisations that expect all their employees

to be infallible. There is no doubt at all, however, that it helps your credibility and standing to be right regularly, right most of the time and, best of all perhaps, right more than people expect—more than your peers and even more than your boss. If you promote a scheme or an idea, which gains approval, is adopted and proves successful, you will at least, collect some of the glory. Of course, you may have to share it with others involved and doing so gracefully—whilst making quietly sure that you do get more than your fair share—is the best tactic for the office politician.

If, on the other hand, you advocate a course of action which is ditched in favour of something else, you get neither thanks nor accolades for saying, "I told you so." In order to maintain an impression of both omniscience and omnipotence, you need to hold back on some things to keep your powder dry on others and perhaps take secret council on those on which you are not, as yet, expert.

> 66 If nobody ever said anything unless he knew what he was talking about, a ghastly hush would descend on the earth. 99
>
> *Sir Alan Herbert*

There are a number of techniques which can help you appear authoritative whilst helping you keep your options open. For example, it is often prudent to phrase remarks you make on topics where you, in fact, know little or nothing, in the form of a question. So instead of saying "Something has to be done about morale in this company," you say "Don't you think something needs to be done about the morale in this company?" Better still, raise several questions: "That proposition raises three key questions ..." Always ask key questions incidentally. It may in fact raise none, or at least no key ones, but it gives you a moment to think as you run down the list.

Hedging can come over as a useful way of implying proper considered caution, rather than you refusing to commit. Though it may very well and quite sensibly do the latter. Thus, phrases like "It seems to me ..." (when it does not), "I'm inclined to think ..." (when perhaps you are not) and "Perhaps there is something to be said for ..." (although there clearly is not), can all be useful to introduce a view from which you can easily disassociate yourself if needs be.

When you do want to sound certain, even though you are anything but, remember that confidence promotes conviction. Say anything with enough clout and even the most arrant nonsense will be taken as gospel. If in doubt adopt Goebbels' philosophy that anything said three times is true, and repeat it—with increasing conviction each time.

Another tactic is to play for time. Suggest a break in a meeting or conversation. Suggest another, later meeting. Suggest a working party to look into the matter. Justify this with a phrase like "This issue is always much more complicated than most people allow" and you will retain your credibility and stay out of trouble. Overall, cultivate the ability to keep your options open until circumstances make it essential to commit.

66 Nothing succeeds like reputation. **99**

John Huston

Two halves make a hole

Before concluding this section, there is one other factor worth mentioning. Amongst the features that categorise those around you in the organisation, is one that really sorts the men from the boys as it were. This is a rather contrived way of drawing attention to the fact that of the people in most organisations, some are men and some are women.

Whichever you are, you cannot afford to alienate the other half, or you may be left with a large hole in the list of allies you hope to assemble. Yet it is not easy. For men, the line between being entirely reasonable and polite or thought to be male chauvinist or patronising to women, can be a narrow one. For women who, rightly or wrongly, have to fight harder to get on in most organisations, there are other traps. You would not want to be seen as the token woman nor as a 'soft touch'. Any particular line can be deployed usefully on occasions, and many men may seek to impress some other man by treating a woman as less than professional. Similarly, a woman may play on her apparent helplessness or good looks to obtain assistance or favours. Any such approach can be taken to extremes—it was the pop singer Madonna who is reputed to have said, "Losing my virginity was a career move"—(Oh if only Susie in Accounts was more ambitious!). For either sex, the job is to maintain a balanced approach and achieve the relationships you want around the organisation regardless of sex.

66 In the sex-war, thoughtlessness is the weapon of the male, vindictiveness of the female. 99

Cyril Connolly

66 On one issue at least, men and women agree: they both distrust women. 99

H.L. Mencken

Ten ways of delaying things (still further)

- Go on holiday.
- Sleep on it.
- Commission some research.
- Call another meeting.
- Refer it to a higher authority.
- Postpone it until after the "busy period".
- Convene a new committee or study group.
- Suggest financing something from next year's budget.
- Write a memo canvassing opinions (and circulate it widely.)
- Say, "Let me think about it for a little longer, it is an important project."

Key guidelines to success

- *Go for one objective at a time.* Trying to do too much at once risks not actually achieving anything at all. Like the juggler who has too many balls in the air, the danger is not so much of dropping one, but of dropping all the balls. If you successfully achieve one thing, then you can simply go on to the next.

- *There is more than one way to skin a cat.* Faced with an obstinent reaction, there are always two ways to proceed. The danger is that the obvious or first thought may not be the one that works nor is it the easier one. Do not get locked into pursuing a dead end. Keep an open and creative mind, and look for an alternative.

- *Aim at the right level.* Ultimately, you have to get right to the real decision maker. 'Gatekeepers' can open doors but that may be all they can do (though sometimes they will promise more).

- *Give credit.* One of the most successful ploys is to persuade people not that what you want is a good idea but, that it is their idea.

- *Keep close to home.* Act on your own ground—for example, holding meetings in your office—whenever possible.

- *Play down the opposition.* In other words, it can sometimes be better to treat another's idea lightly rather than respond with a serious argument. A 'not that old idea again' sort of comment can work wonders.

Next we take the warfare analogy a little further and investigate a number of issues to help us fight—or defend—our corner.

06

Knives and Other Weapons

> **66** The weak have one weapon; the errors of those who think they are strong. **99**
>
> *Georges Bidoult*

All the things there are

As we have seen already, the organisational world is something of a jungle, and one with a hostile element to it. Those who survive in the jungle do so by utilising every feature of the environment to their advantage. The very same principle applies in the office. You have to use everything around you, everything that happens and everyone with whom you interact, to aid your cause. What kind of thing? Well, everything from computers to training courses, from written reports to research. The trick is first, spot what can be used to your advantage and then to extract the best from it. The following examples—by no means a comprehensive lot (make your own and think broadly)—will be both illustrative of the kind of thing that can be used to good effect, and how such effect can be obtained.

Whoops!

You may just have noticed that office life does not always run smoothly all the time. In fact, if we are honest, its path is regularly strewn with disasters of one sort or another.

Some may be comparatively minor. For instance your failure to complete a task or complete the writing of a document on time —"Sorry, the report on improving office efficiency is late because I inadvertently wiped the text off the word processor, either through momentary inattention, or monumental cock-up." Such disaster-through-delay is an all too frequent occurrence in most offices. How many things are you waiting for, right now, that are overdue? How many other people are holding you up? And who, as a result, thinks that you equate the word 'urgency' with 'mañana'?

At the other end of the scale are major catastrophes. They may be major in themselves: the new product is late— and the launch advertising breaks are scheduled tomorrow; the dispatch department just went on strike again. Or, they may be smaller but major in impact: the client's name is misspelt on a vital proposal; the product name, now printed on tens of thousands of packs ready to be shipped overseas means 'bum' in Korean. Then there are the real 22 carrot catastrophes, those that have dire consequences throughout the organisation and leave no one unaffected—like many a computer system error or when the tea lady resigns.

In addition to all these, there are those cumulative disasters where one seemingly insignificant thing leads to another and another and—but you know the kind of thing—someone's train to work is late (only an hour); some miss the meeting on office reorganisation (never mind, it is a committee of 14); someone is unable to remind the group of the fact that four new people join their department in a month's time (no great harm done, surely?). Then things move on apace, plans are drawn up, furniture is ordered, moving arrangements made, memos written, telephones scheduled for relocation. A little time later when the detailed schedule is circulated, it is immediately discovered that accommodation in that one department is insufficient. The whole plan has to be redesigned and someone is saying, "You never told me."

Whatever the nature of any disaster however, there will always be an opportunity lurking about there somewhere for someone to spot and take advantage of for his own advancement. Blame will be allocated, someone will have to pick up the pieces and there will be credit to be gained once things are finally sorted out. Not just "Well done", but, "Well done, I don't know how you managed to sort all that out after the initial mess George left you."

So, whatever happens and however much damage may have been done, look on the bright side: there may just be something positive you can pull from the wreckage.

> 66 Things are going to get a lot worse before they get worse. 99
>
> *Lili Tomlin*

The office marriage

There can be no doubt that a secretary, or at least a good one, is one of your most important allies in the office war. She—it is most often she (though it was only the presence of a male secretary in my own office some years back that prompted the dropping of the expression 'the girls' in favour of 'the support staff')—is an invaluable asset in a number of ways.

First, she can make your job easier. Second, she can act in a key ambassadorial role so that others are more aware of your talents and achievements. And third, she can forestall or camouflage your inadequacies. Ideally, she will do all three. Mind you, finding someone that can contribute to this extent is not easy. Some potential (actual?) secretaries have trouble contributing a reasonable standard and measure of even the most basic office skills like 'Fastan d accurATE tiping' (you see, the poor ones get in everywhere). Others are at the other extreme. There is a story about a busy senior executive, always on the go, regularly out of the office and often out of the country. One day a colleague comes to his office hoping to see him. "Sorry," says his secretary, "he is in Hong Kong until Monday." "Away again," says the colleague. "Tell me, who does all his work when he's away from the office?" The secretary looks him straight in the eye and replies, "The same person who does it when he's here." Whilst not all secretaries take over to that extent—though some do mine assures me—all can help those wanting to win the business battle.

The ideal secretary needs a daunting range of attributes. These include a memory like an elephant, eyes at the back of her head, high degree of tact, charm and loyalty, and a degree of appropriate ability. If others refer to her as a first class secretary, then this will reflect well on you. The ideal situation comes about in two ways: what she does and how she looks.

Take appearance first. There are those who, uncertain who to hire when recruiting, simply opt for the best-looking candidate. This may work. There are, after all, those who not only look attractive, but work well too. But this is not always the case. They may spend all their time on the phone talking to their boyfriend or in deep discussion with their colleagues as to why they are still unattached at the ripe age of 22. Even if it does work, perhaps another more senior member of the organisation may immediately poach them. Others opt for the older women, more experienced, more reliable; or with more bad habits and a lifetime of dramas to recount and friends to telephone.

Perhaps avoiding anything to excess may be the best line.

Pick a candidate who is not so good looking that her desk is constantly surrounded by all the young bucks of the organisation and no work is done, or so unattractive that no one wants to walk past her to see you at all. Do recognise though that anything like this is highly likely to cause trouble!

The appearance, from a work point of view is, in any case, much more important. Does she look efficient? Is her work area kept tidy? It will show you up if she does and you do not. On the other hand, if you are pleading overwork and she is so tidy that she appears to have little of substance to do, that will not help either. Just as important, does she have the confidence and weight to act on your behalf? Can she say "No" when necessary—"No, he is not available at the moment" when you are trying to think. "No, that report is not ready yet..." giving a good reason why which or who does not blame you. And can she not just say "No", but "NO!" and make it sound firm. She must be on your side. If she sees herself as your eyes and ears, if she sees herself as helping to determine what others think of you and what you do, if she works with you rather than for you, then you will have a head start on anyone without the same degree of support.

This may all sound rather cosy and straightforward. Recruit the right person and you have a built-in lifetime support. Not so. Ignoring the difficulty of recruiting them, secretaries are like the rarest of orchids. They need constant care and attention and even then they are apt to flower at the wrong moment. But the process is worthwhile. Look after them. Remember, trust and loyalty are both two-way streets. Give time to the relationship. Hold regular meetings and communicate regularly and well. A secretary constantly saying, "They never tell me anything," is not likely to give others a good impression of you. Give them some real responsibility and then perhaps you will have a friend and ally for life, or at least for a year or three.

In addition, you will probably have started a few rumours, and your spouse will be deeply suspicious of the whole thing. Never mind, you do not spend so much time with them.

Meglomania Case No 8: Do remember this is Confidential

Gerald had been with Megalomania for many years. As Finance Director he felt, with some justification, that he had done an excellent job of steering the company financially in a way that had made or protected very large amounts of money. Yet when the call came from the Headhunters he was not only flattered, he was tempted. His feelings of frustration about many of the organisation's recent activities came to the surface. He went off to the interview determined to make a good impression. And he did.

After the interview, he had to provide more information about himself. Taking his secretary, Pamela, into his confidence, he told her of the situation and instructing her to say nothing, he asked her to type up a new Curriculum Vitae

The following week a major crisis blew up. A subsidiary company hit problems. Worse, there was confusion about some of the figures. The wrong information had been passed out from the Headquarters (H.Q.), by Gerald himself, and this delayed key decisions and made the situation worse.

The last thing Gerald wanted, as a new potential employer considered whether to offer him a considerable opportunity and lift in salary, was any doubts cast on his abilities. So, when the Managing Director (M.D.) came on demanding to know what had gone wrong, Gerald tactically indicated that just filed away, the M.D. told his secretary, she told someone else and … some time later, Pamela discovered what had happened and started to worry about her reputation. After all, with her boss apparently leaving, her job was suddenly not looking so secure.

Some time later still, Gerald had a letter from the Headhunters. They were still most impressed with his abilities, but … the sting in the tail … another candidate evidently had the edge on him.

Thereafter, a great deal of wondering went on. Gerald wondered if he would have got the job if his M.D. had not found out, in the wrong way and at the wrong time, what he was planning and tried to queer the pitch with the other firm. He silently vowed never to trust Pamela again. The M.D. wondered if he wanted an unhappy Finance Director on an ongoing basis. And Pamela wondered about whether she could go on working for someone who publicly blamed her for his errors, and whether, after the events since she let slip that she had heard he was moving on, he would want her to anyway.

A general unease became the order of the day.

<u>Moral</u>: Trust is a two-way street and anything else tends to lead to trouble and make events even more unpredictable than usual.

A bit of a do

The office politicians need not necessarily be the life and soul of the party, though they are unlikely to be shrinking violets either. There are certain events, social events that is, that slip into the corporate calendar and about which the more politically astute need to take a view. Some may be celebrations. A retirement party perhaps. You may be only too glad to see the back of the person retiring, but most often it pays to be present and magnanimous. It may even be that volunteering to say a few words, and doing so nicely, will score you a few points—"That was a nice tribute, and I wasn't sure they got on."

Rather different are the ritual events—the office party at Christmas or New Year perhaps. Incidentally, never ever ever volunteer to organise such an event. You will never please everyone and the worst excesses of anyone who misbehaves may well be left at your door.

The date is set, the food—and of course the drink—is ordered. There is sufficient for everyone to get a little tipsy, not so much as to constitute a benefit that attracts tax. You have decided to attend. You are looking forward to it. Really. Besides, it provides an unmissable opportunity to kiss Mary from Accounts or the Managing Director (a choice dependent on your inclination, courage or level of intoxication as well as sexual orientation). Remember what fun it was last year? Or do you still have the scars?

But it is not all fun and games on such occasions. There are serious decisions to be made. For example, at Christmas, what should be sent to key customers? Years ago, it was no problem. If they had no outstanding invoices, they got a card (usually one chosen by the Managing Director's wife, who is well known for her impeccable taste). If not, then the card went out with a reminder of any debt. For the most important customers, those whose orders really could not be done without, they would be invited in for a small glass of warm sherry and something to nibble off a stick. This, of course, on a different occasion from the office party and with Mary from Accounts safely hidden away.

66 The cocktail party is easily the worst invention since castor oil. 99

Elsa Maxwell

In today's competitive times a more tangible 'Thank you' may be necessary. Not just anything, something with the expensively designed corporate logo tastefully featured on it as a permanent reminder of the organisation and all its works. The question is, What? And, worse, who should decide? Something useful perhaps—though it is difficult to think of anything new. But what if they notice amongst their various gifts that nothing has come from your organisation? Not good for your image. Alternatively, they can be sent something like a bottle of Scotch, though this has the habit of disappearing by Boxing Day and leaving not even a fleeting reminder of the organisation in their mind. To make a real impression, you need to be creative, to splash out and spend enough to get recipients to say "Wow!" It needs some objective research. You might do worse than to send a sample of anything you are thinking of using to an objective person for an external impartial opinion. I can do this if you wish. As a suggestion of the kind of things that I would be happy to check (though not, of course, return), there is a laptop computer, a Porsche ... even a new leather briefcase would be nice. There is no need to put the logo on; you can rely on my feedback.

I have digressed somewhat but nevertheless, the point remains that on any occasion that is marked by the organisation, you need to think about your role in it. As with anything else there are opportunities for some in any event. Keep your eyes open, stay sufficiently sober and who knows what the outcome will be.

Cooking the books

It would be nice if the organisation you work for is able to proceed on its way with no concern for sordid financial matters. Few, if any, organisations have this luxury. For most people, there is a budget to be considered; for many, there are targets to be hit. It is very useful to win control over one or two central budgets. Maybe 'Research', 'Contingencies' or nicely amorphous areas like 'Travel and Entertaining' might have your name on; anywhere that has reasonable funds and such a miscellany of items going into it that items of individual expenditure get lost. If you have control, not responsibility of course, just an ability to charge things to such a heading, gives you an additional area of power. This not only means that you can lose various sums of money you have clocked up yourself but that you can, on occasions, offer it as a repository for selected items of expenditure to other carefully chosen people. "Give me that invoice", you say magnanimously, "and I will put it down as 'Research'. " And you note another favour owed and resolve to call it in in due course.

Budgets on the other hand have a tiresome habit of regularly drawing attention to the state of play in your department. Luckily such documents are understood in their entirety by few people and are in any case, subject to a variety of interpretations. There are budgets ... and budgets. Some will show the picture of how things were six weeks ago; some show the approximate position; some the predicted position—say, in six weeks time; some show the position as you would like it to be, others as someone else would like it to be. Still others show part of the position, as it is but without this or that, or as it will be when this or that is added. Or it may show the position compared favourably with last month's or last year's. Just describing all these make clear the complications inherent in such situations. If you are reasonably numerate, and quick on your feet, this list is almost endless. Beyond all these, there is finally the budget that shows what the position actually is. When all is going fine you can dispense with all the other versions and simply use this. If not, pause for a moment and list some multipurpose excuses.

Remember too that it is said that there are two kinds of manager with regard to budgets: those who go over them carefully every month, and those who just go over them.

> 66 Just about the time you think you can make both ends meet, somebody moves the ends. 99
> *Pansy Penner*

Before leaving the topic of finances, an anecdote about numeracy comes to mind.

A group of managers attended a training course. The course was a general management programme. One course participant could not get anything right regarding finance and by the time the course concluded, he was very much the class 'dunce'. As attendees dispersed back to their respective companies the group agreed to meet up a year later to see how everyone was faring and in due course, a dinner was arranged at a smart restaurant. The 'dunce' arrived a little late but as he did so it was clear to all, from the Porsche he parked outside, the suit he wore and a dozen other signs of affluence, that he was doing very well for himself.

"I would never have thought it possible," said the course tutor. "Tell us, what have you been up to since the course?" "It wasn't easy," he replied. "I was laid off by my employer soon after the course finished. I then tried various different things without much success, so I finally started up in business myself—in the import/export business in Africa. I discovered that I could buy things for $2 on one side of the border and sell them for $4 on the other. It's gone well, I'm still amazed at how that two per cent adds up."

This is not at all, you will of course have spotted, how percentages work. But sometimes perhaps formal understanding of figures and finance is less important than the flair to make it work!

> 66 The safest way to double your money is to fold it over once and put it in your pocket. 99
>
> *Kin Hubbard*

The longer or shorter course

There was a time when those who succeeded in business did so with no more than their native wit and perhaps a few basic exams passed. These days, even the most mundane office jobs seem to require a degree in something or another, and you have to be numerate, computer literate and able to operate proactively (whenever did we come to see anything wrong with simply being active?) and synergistically as well. What is more—tomorrow, there will doubtlessly be a whole new battery of techniques to take on board and get into your armoury. The trouble is that keeping up to date is rather more complex than reading the occasional magazine article, or asking good old Fred how it is done. You have to take active steps (proactive ones even) to ensure you are, and will remain, sufficiently qualified for the job. You may need to go on a course for a day or two or a few weeks or months and do so on a regular basis.

However, if your boss tells you to go on a course, be wary. It is possible that he wants you out of the way for a while. If he asks you if you would like to go on a course, still be wary. This may be just a way of getting you out of the way without you becoming suspicious.

On the other hand, such attendance may be a genuine opportunity. You may learn something new or even something new and important. Alternatively, just being reminded of something important can be useful, or being helped to reorder your priorities. All this may help you do your job better, and if so, that can help you survive and prosper. So the sensible office politician takes a positive view of training (indeed, as a trainer, it seems to me that *everyone* should take a positive view of training).

In addition, there may be advantages beyond what you learn about the subject of the course. You may meet someone who will be a valuable future contact. If you can decide the time at which you attend, you may contrive to miss something within the organisation—a meeting, a social event, or an inquest. You may be able to use the fact of attendance to delay some hated project ... "Surely it would be better to decide that after the course ..." You can blame unpopular ideas or measures on the course tutor ... "Well, that is what we were recommended to do, and he should know..." Perhaps, there will be a course photo or other memento that can usefully be displayed in your office or at least, an impressive course binder to add to your bookshelf.

Further, there may be other benefits. Perhaps it will be held somewhere nice—a smart hotel in an attractive location or even overseas—in an attractive city, or on a beautiful beach. On the other hand, you could be unlucky and find yourself somewhere much less attractive. The odds are not good. For every course held overlooking an idyllic croquet lawn (in the U.K. all course venues have a croquet lawn, where, if you have not played it before, you will discover it is the most cut-throat game known to man, a cross between snooker and cock fighting) there are 10 that are held in second rate hotels. These tend to be close to a noisy main road, just outside some miserable town and do not make for a memorable experience. Some training managers are such cheapskates. Even when the venue is pleasant, there may be hazards. One company sent a team of people to a good venue in the wilds of the English countryside. On the first night it snowed. Three weeks later they finally got out, two weeks late, two stone overweight and knowing the topic of the course and their fellow attendees rather better than anyone had ever dreamt, or most of them would have wished.

You need to pick the right course. One that is conducted by an organisation whose kudos will reflect well on you. Ashridge or Cranfield management colleges in the U.K. or Harvard in the U.S.A., perhaps. And of course, you cannot go wrong with a company like Touchstone Training & Consultancy (sorry, but if I did not take the opportunity to plug my own operation in such a book as this, I should not be writing it!).

If, by any chance, you have not asked to attend any courses recently, then start putting in requests at once. There is no harm in being seen to seek to improve your, no doubt, already considerable talents and, as has been said, attendance may represent a real opportunity. Bear in mind, however, the old saying mentioned earlier that 'the trouble with opportunities is that they are so often come disguised ... as hard work'. These days most courses are just that, particularly residential ones where you may find yourself slaving over a hot syndicate at midnight, with a presentation still to prepare for delivery first thing in the morning. But then nothing is ever for nothing, isn't it?

A day or two away on a course is one thing; a whole degree course is quite another, particularly if you are already working and previously felt you had left education behind for good. Yet a surprisingly large number of people go back as it were—to school. Some of them go back and manage to get their organisation to pay for the cost. Which sounds like a neat trick if you can do it, and, of course, if you can also succeed in returning to work a year later or whatever without losing your place on a rung or two of the ladder.

Is it worthwhile? Well …

> 66 Sending men into war without training them is like abandoning them. 99
>
> *Confucius*

None the wiser

There is a story told of a complex trial where a particularly tedious expert witness was giving interminable and impenetrable evidence. When at last he had finished, the bemused, bored and irritable judge leaned forward, "I have to say that I am none the wiser for that." "Maybe not," replied the expert witness with some presence of mind. "But you are much better informed." So it is with business qualifications. Some people emerge from the management colleges full of knowledge, but sometimes no better in terms of what they can do and how well they can do it. Most management jobs are essentially practical—hands-on in some respect. Marketing people have to be able to relate to markets and deliver the profits; production people sort the technical problems and so on. Being a business graduate does not guarantee that you can achieve anything. Indeed, it is perhaps worth repeating (from my book *Marketing stripped bare*) a story that illustrates how nevertheless, these marketing graduates can have an inflated idea of their own worth. It is like the man who claimed to have found the perfect new business venture—

something guaranteed to maximise profit. It consisted of buying MBAs for what they are worth and selling them for what they think they are worth. Despite this thought, business qualifications surely matter but they are not a guarantee of anything nor do they allow you to make automatic judgements about others.

Whatever practical value some qualifications have, they do, undeniably, have status value. Or some do. Harvard is probably still the leader. Some of the European business schools, like INSEAD and IMEDE have a cache of their own. A number in the U.K. are now very respectable. And around Asia numbers of institutions offer impressive qualifications or a way of studying for overseas ones while remaining in *situ*. A degree from one of the best establishments counts for a lot; even a visit to such an establishment, perhaps for a short course, can be useful, leading to conversations which start "When I was at ..." And a note in your CV and perhaps visible souvenirs of your visit. It is best to play it a little bit safe and not claim too much. Certainly, you need to know the basic facts about where you have been if your visit was fleeting. If you did a course at INSEAD you will have had to speak some French. Do you? If you were at Henley, remember that is the one by the U.K.'s River Thames and so on.

Such exposure does produce some useful trappings. People will notice the ties, badges, invitations to class reunions—though they may comment, "It was how long ago?" And, as the majority of people have not had the luxury of such a period, yours makes a point. One individual achieved the ultimate point scoring moment following an invitation to conduct a guest lecture at a prestigious establishment. On his visit he was given a windscreen sticker to display in his car to secure access to the car park. Some time later, a business colleague noticed this, mentioned that he had attended a course there himself and asked whether his colleague had done so too. "No," he was able to reply. "I was running one." (It is a while ago so maybe I should take the sticker out of my car now).

> 66 People at the top of the tree are those without the qualifications to detain them at the bottom. 99
>
> *Peter Ustinov*

How am I doing?

Many people would agree that one of their least favourite moments of the year is their annual job appraisal. Many managers are not too keen on conducting these annual, or sometimes more frequent, rituals. The worst managers hate doing them because they are downright bad at doing them and at worst, because they are unsure how to go about them. Sometimes they are just embarrassing, contrived, ill-structured witch hunts: a chance for past sins to be revisited and for managers to make themselves feel powerful by indulging in extensive criticism.

They should, however, be valuable. They should focus on improving performance in the future. And no astute office politician should ignore the opportunity that they afford.

So, let us start by considering their purpose. An appraisal should act to:

- Review individuals' past performance
- Plan future work, work emphasis and overall role
- Set specific goals at an individual level
- Agree and thus create individual ownership for such goals, making them more likely to be achieved
- Provide appropriate on-the-spot coaching
- Prompt action in training and development (and the identification of what may be useful), and thus maintain, enhance and add to skills
- Obtain feedback
- Reinforce and strengthen working relationships
- Act as a catalyst to delegation
- Highlight long term career intentions
- Heighten motivation and commitment

This is what appraisals should do. They should not be an ego trip for power crazy managers, nor should they be rushed through just to 'get them out of the way'. These intentions are not mutually exclusive, though the emphasis may be more on some than others.

Overall, the intention is clear: it is to act as a catalyst to making future performance better than—or simply different from—that of the past. This may sometimes involve identifying and correcting personal weaknesses, but it is just as likely that changes in the environment or the organisation's intentions make changes to what is done, and how things are done, necessary. Appraisal should never be seen as a witch-hunt, and the concentration should always be on the positive.

That said, how can an appraisal do anything but help? If it shows you how to avoid mistakes, acts to help you do better in future and acts also as a spur to development equipping you with new or enhanced skills, is that not beneficial not only to how you perform your job, but also to you and your career?

The intentions of an appraisal scheme must be clear. To achieve this, and to focus the discussion at an appraisal meeting suitably, many organisations will have a prescribed, documented and systematic approach. This often takes the form of a structured format that lists the areas of planned discussion, and that usually includes an element of evaluation to measure, objectively, past performance. Whatever is used make sure you are familiar with it. If ratings are seen in such a 'means to an end' way, then there is no reason why they should cause problems.

The secret to making your appraisal successful is, in a word, preparation. You can play an active role in making sure you get the most from your meeting.

As has been said, you must know the agreed system and the areas of activity to be addressed. You need to be ready and able to participate in a constructive analysis and discussion. Thus, preparation is much more than simply 'thinking about the meeting' just ahead of it taking place.

Appraisal is a pulling together of thought and analysis that goes on through the year; or which should do. So preparation needs to be spread over the long term as well. It is useful to keep a file and make notes progressively about areas that seem to be going to be worth discussing. Often, topics for discussion will, in any case, be the subject of ongoing review and action. In that case the appraisal will act as a review of progress to date and to highlight future needs rather than being a starting point.

Immediate preparation is important too. An appraisal meeting, like any other, needs a considered agenda (which relates carefully to timing) and this should be as much the responsibility of you as appraisee as of anyone else. There is a danger of feeling nothing is really necessary but to 'play it by ear', especially if people involved know each other well and instinctively opt for informality. If there is anything you are not sure of, talk to your appraiser about it ahead of the formal meeting. Certainly, make absolutely sure that you have the agenda for the meeting far enough ahead to prepare properly.

66 I can take any amount of criticism, as long as it is unqualified praise. 99

Noel Coward

Given these preliminary considerations, the meeting, which might typically last from perhaps 90 minutes to a whole morning, should go smoothly. Though this can only be the case provided the attitude of those involved is positive and constructive, and this in turn will tend to relate to the overall organisational that prevails.

In addition, three overriding principles are paramount. It is in the nature of a successful appraisal that:

- during the meeting the appraisee does most of the talking (though the appraiser may need to chair the meeting)
- the focus and weight of time and discussion is on the future more than the past (the two go together, of course, but the end results are actions for the future, albeit stemming, in part, from the experience of the period just gone)
- they must be given sufficient time (typically more than an hour, sometimes a whole morning)

Thus the appraisal that is half an hour of ill prepared and random grousing or which focuses primarily on one, usually negative, thing from the past is not ideal. Furthermore, a constructive appraisal will spark ideas—it should have a creative element—and for these and other agreed actions firm follow up should be insisted upon. You should make sure, in other words, that things agreed on actually happen and that timings are broadly kept to—an urgent requirement for you to attend a time management course, for example, should not still be pending in six months time.

Remember that even the best performances can be improved. Even the most expert and competent people—yes, you too—have new things to learn and new ways to adopt; the dynamic environment in which we all work sees to that. To summarise, the appraisal process is not all about criticism and highlighting errors or faults (though realistically some of that may need doing). It is about using analysis and discussion to take matters forward. It is about building on success. It is about sharing good experience and effective approaches and, above all, it is about making more of the future.

It is not being unreasonably political to insist your appraisal is given due consideration. If, in the event, you do not find it constructive, then something is wrong. So too, if you are a manager and appraise other people. Asked to list the desirable characteristics in a boss, people put as one of the highest, "That they are someone I learn from." Make your people enjoy their appraisals and find them useful and they will love you for it.

> **66** It is what you learn after you know it all that counts. **99**
>
> *John Wooden*

The small print

However optimistic you are about your prospects of winning the office war, it is always advisable to have a little insurance. If things were to go wrong—if you were to emerge not on top of the heap but in it—how will that leave you? A week's notice and the company car goes back at the start of the week? Or could it leave you with a golden handshake, able to keep the car and with enough money in hand to consider retiring rather than looking for other employment?

This presents something of a quandary. You are unlikely to get the right sort of contract early on in your career, as you are not sufficiently valuable. On the other hand once you are a bigger fish there may well be others around who would rather you were not so well locked in. This is one of those Catch 22 situations to which there is no easy answer. Indeed, there may be no answer at all. If you see a moment when it is right to demand the earth with a 100 per cent chance of success, seize the moment; and let the rest of us know when such a moment may occur.

Contracts and terms is not an area where you can rely on good intentions and vague promises. As the old saying goes—'A verbal agreement is not worth the paper it is written on'—and there are those who will recommend getting the lawyers in to verify the handshake (and count the fingers afterwards). You need to look very carefully at what your contract of employment says. Not just at the obvious bits—four weeks holiday and details of things like health insurance and pension—but at the small print.

In due course your considerations may need to include more weighty matters: so called golden handshakes (bonus payments to attract people into a new job) and golden handcuffs (incentives to keep you there). Nowhere should there be any clause (sic) for concern.

> 66 Contract: an agreement that is binding only on the weaker party. 99
>
> *Frederick Sawyer*

Megalomania Case No 9: Timing is everything

Megalomania has a large Publicity Department. This met regularly for so called 'ideas sessions', and never were these sessions more important than when sales were down. Alec had only been with the firm a short while, but it so happened that his attendance at his first ideas session coincided with a real emergency. Sales of one particular product were well down, and, with stock literally backing up in the warehouse, everyone—but everyone—was demanding that Publicity come up with some magic new scheme that would get sales moving and people off other peoples' backs.

The meeting reviewed both what was being done already and considered new ideas fielded as it progressed by members of the department. It seemed to Alec that many wheels were being reinvented, but no one had the answer.

With the benefit of outside experience, he felt the real problem was that the product was not getting well displayed. What seemed to be needed was a promotion to the dealers to encourage proper display rather than to the customers encouraging them to buy something they currently could not see in the shops. This also had the merit of being able to be more quickly implemented than some of the other ideas.

Despite his being new to the company, Alec was asked what ideas he had. He asked a few questions; he made a few comments on some of the other ideas; but made no mention of the scheme that he in fact thought best. The meeting broke up largely undecided and a date was set for another session to follow soon.

Alec now set to do his homework inside and outside the company: he checked and consulted so that he could refine and write up his scheme. He circulated a paper ahead of the next meeting date.

The meeting began in a state of some desperation. Sales were still down. Demands for action were up. Early on, the department head asked Alec to say a little more about his idea. He immediately collected a number of criticisms. Surely, it could not be solved so simply; surely, they had done this before—In effect—the answer could not lie with a newcomer, or if it did, then how did it reflect on the other members of the team?

Because the idea was thought through, because it was well documented, opinion came to be in favour. The head of the department finally called for the immediate implementation, and Alec was in for thanks and a major part in the scheme almost before he had his feet under the desk.

As he had also thought about how others could work with him on the implementation, he carried most people with him rather than being resented as being too clever by half.

Not a bad start; particularly as the scheme worked well.

<u>Moral</u>: Pick your time (and do your homework). Alec could have raised the idea at the first meeting, but the chances were that it would either not have found favour, or that discussion would have developed the i

dea into something no longer associated with him. At the second meeting the scene was set, the need was more urgent and the time was right.

A word with the judge

In an ever more litigious world another route to success and riches has opened up. You take your employer to court and you sue them for damages. Even if you have cause, and some employers are pigs that deserve to be sued to the ends of the Earth, this cannot be all plain sailing. Say you successfully win damages because your boss is unreasonable in some way. You win. You pocket some money. What happens next? You go into the office the next day, your boss welcomes you with open arms and everything continues as per normal (with your boss curbing whatever unreasonable behaviour upset you in the first place). I do not think so. It is more likely that nothing will ever be the same again; not least your prospects for promotion.

This may not be fair or right. So much in life is unfair that this may not surprise you (I mean how could Jennifer Aniston not even know me, much less want me? Sorry, I digress.), but it is likely to reflect reality. Things will not be the same. There are, of course, numbers of things that occur within organisations that are not only wrong, but which are also illegal. An employee should not be discriminated on grounds of race, creed or sexuality. They should even be left alone for wearing a ring in their nose, though I for one would not want to work alongside them. They should not be harassed or bullied. And, seriously, I do not condone for a single second such practices.

Sometimes such things are minor and can be dealt with via a little internal discipline or with just a word. When, if, they are serious, and there is no excuse for them, then they need dealing with, but you should not get involved without due consideration of the consequences. On the one hand, action needs to be taken to nip such things in the bud, on the other it may be politic to play a careful game with such matters.

As an example of the scale all this has taken on, I noticed, as I wrote this, a story in the newspapers about a lawsuit brought against an investment bank, Dresdner Keinwork Wasserstein (and no, it is not an attempt to get the name changed to something a little more catchy). Six women employed by the company are suing their employer for £1.6 billion. Yes, £1.6 billion! The newspaper reported that they allege that they were bullied and degraded by such behaviour as their male colleagues taking clients to strip clubs and bringing prostitutes into the office. Not behaviour that many people would regard as particularly seemly perhaps, and I am all for such things being stamped on, but do you really need such an obscene amount of money to get over the trauma? Though the detail of their allegations include one of them being referred to as the 'Pamela Anderson of trading', and having someone say, about a box of chocolates, that she should move it off her desk before any of the men had their 'hands in her box'. Well! How terrible. Is having such a lamentable sense of humour really a matter for legal action? Watch the news. It may be a route is opening up for you too.

This is an area to view with considerable care. It is possible to make a killing, but still ends up dead from a career progression perspective. After all if the last item on your CV catalogues your record in the courts—damages for someone touching your knee; more damages for the stress involved in being called an incompetent nincompoop when you inadvertently allowed the factory to grind to a halt for a day and half; and more damages still for failing to be promoted even though the rival candidate made you look like a bumbling amateur—then it is hardly likely to mark you down with a potential new employer as the ideal, hassle free candidate.

Game, set and match

Successful office politicians come in all shapes and sizes. They operate at all levels of the organisation, either because everyone has to start somewhere, or because they have set their sights lower than the top (This, of course, does not make them any less political, there may be plenty of things they still want to achieve). They all have in common, however, the ability first to spot things around them that might help their cause; and secondly to think of ways of exploiting such things.

In this respect—if not always in others—they are decisive. Unlike the manager who was said to have a brilliant mind—until he made it up—such people spot the opportunity for advantage and run with it. They see opportunities in everything.

Take research, for instance. This is an invaluable process for the office politician to get involved in. It takes so long.

It costs so much. Its findings can be so involved. So where are the opportunities? Well, for a start it is a classic reason to delay. You can suggest commissioning some research first, before proceeding. You can wait until the results are available, analysed or interpreted. You can suggest that the findings are ambiguous and thus commissioning more research is only sensible, or you can simply say that the findings need to be digested, or circulated—and all before proceeding further. But delay is not the only possible use of research. It can support your prejudices, confirm pre-agreed decisions or build on an earlier idea. It can show a proposition is untenable, that it is too expensive, will take too long—or is just plain wrong.

> **❝**Of course, we don't know what we are doing. If we knew what we were doing, it would not be research.**❞**
>
> *Albert Einstein*

Alternatively, research can help support a case, it can get what you want approved and under way. Sometimes this may be just what you want.

You can or must, indeed, approach everything in the same way. Asking yourself, how this or that can help you, how it will affect other people; both short term and long term is important. Time scale is particularly important. It is one thing to see that something can have an immediate advantage. Say today or tomorrow. It is another to see that it may hold long term advantage, perhaps a week, a month or a year or more ahead.

The whole process has something in common with a game like chess. In the game staying ahead of your opponent may mean that, as you make a move, you have to think of the next six or 10 subsequent moves or more. The permutations increase depending on the number of moves ahead you are considering; but no one has said the overall process had to be simple. Similarly, a chain of events can be anticipated. People attend a particular meeting; during the meeting they get wind of some event; they check it out later; and as a result, they get involved in something that is a current issue, perhaps joining a committee; on the committee they meet someone new to them within the organisation; that person is involved in something else and gives advance warning of ... and so on, and so on. You have only to think back over past events to see how much in your life is of this nature. Sometimes it seems just happenstance, sometimes you bless the day you consciously took the first step and set the whole chain in motion. And often, when you look at how other people have things organised, you curse their good fortune; but, if you are honest, it is clear that they had it all planned out long ago.

The game in the end goes to the people who handle all this best—those who see something they can get from all the people around them, whatever their position in the hierarchy, whatever their immediate apparent usefulness; those who see possibilities in all the events happening around them, whether expected or unexpected, regular or occasional, creative or boring; and those who look out to the extremities of their vision—inside and outside the organisation.

Every day you must think therefore of what you can

develop from the people and events of that day. From the contents of the post and e-mail in the morning, to lunch in the pub, to the meeting, the new recruit, the reorganisation, the market downturn (or upturn), the item in the internal newsletter, the overheard comment in reception. Such a list could well be virtually endless. It will certainly change. Like everything in office life, the process is dynamic. What is there to be taken advantage of today may not be there tomorrow at all, though something else doubtless will be.

The successful office politicians never cease to take all these in—whilst at the same time appearing to take little interest in such politicking, and appearing simply to concentrate on whatever job they have on hand—so that the success they achieve brings an appropriate degree of recognition and reward, as a foundation for anything else they can bring to bear.

So, ultimately it is down to you. With sufficient ammunition in your armoury and enough people on your side (or at least not actively working against you) things may go well—perhaps surprisingly well. If so, always remember the old saying that 'when things appear to be going well—you have definitely overlooked something'.

There will hopefully be—if you organise your office life as you wish—some moments when all is going well, when the pressure eases, and some time even when you can relax, at least for a while—though it is wisely said that you should never lie down when the vultures are circling overhead. Bear in mind that any safe moments will be few in number, and short, very short.

There will be no moments when you can be safely off-guard.

> **❝**He was a self-made man who owed his lack of success to nobody.**❞**
>
> *Joseph Heller*

Megalomania Case No 10: *Delusions of Adequacy*

Raymond Thomson was Megalomania's Sales Director, a classic 'salesman made good'. He had ridden roughshod over everyone and everything to get to where he is now. He was brash, he was pushy, he was out for himself; but he had drive and initiative and was a very good salesman. On his sales record, he had certainly deserved rapid promotion. As an Area Sales Manager his area had had record sales results—he had sold much of it himself to make sure. He had quickly been appointed National Sales Manager, a position he had only occupied for two months when the unexpected death of the previous Sales Director left him the obvious choice for that role.

However, the job he then had to do was very different from his previous ones. He had to manage a volatile group of Area Managers—all of whom lacked nothing in confidence and some of whom thought his rise through the organisation had been altogether too fast. He had to liaise with a wide range of senior people throughout the organisation and concern himself with long term strategy rather than short term tactics.

None of this played to his strengths. He was not good at distancing himself from his close colleagues on the sales team. He found it difficult to see the large picture and think strategically and far enough ahead; and with all the tact and diplomacy of a sledgehammer, he found that relations with other senior managers and his own staff alike were not as constructive as they should have been. He was a classic case of the 'Peter Principle'—someone who has been promoted to a job which, in fact, he is not qualified to do.

As he began to struggle a little with the new task in front of him; indeed, to admit—at least to himself—that he was struggling...—others, waiting on the sidelines with their own axes to grind, began to recognise an opportunity.

<u>Moral</u>: Indeed, some of those who hold key positions, have real Achilles heels in tackling their jobs. Those who spot them, use these weaknesses to achieve their own ends. Thus, one should beware of biting off more than he can chew. Successful office politicians are realistic about their own limitations.

Ten things that sound certain, definitive and authoritative (but are sometimes not)

- "This is my final word."
- "This is the last time."
- "There is no more money."
- "I will consider it carefully."
- "The research confirms it."

- "That's the policy."
- "It is down here in black and white."
- "It is a matter of principle."
- "Yes."
- "No."

Key guidelines to success

- *Keep up the pressure.* The greater the stress people are under, the more it becomes difficult for them to think clearly, not to over-react and to keep their cool. Perhaps there are moments when you can supply a little of the stress. (And, of course, moments when you will do better by keeping your own cool).

- *Beware of a funny thing happening...* Humour needs handling with care. It can lighten a difficult moment but there are dangers—for instance, mocking humour (and some of your opposition doubtless so deserve it) can rebound, producing sympathy for those so mocked (though in your view they will manifestly not deserve it).

- *Never cut off options until you have to.* Whilst a range of possible courses of action are possible, do not be hasty to rule out any of them—even those that do not appear promising. If you did that before circumstances have changed, you may find you have removed a bolthole or a winning stroke. Closing off options too soon can be a major cause of difficulty.

- *Always appear genuine.* It is said that if you can fake the sincerity, then everything else is easy.

07

Will You be Successful at Office Politics?

66 Whom the gods wish to destroy they first call promising. 99

Cyril Connolly

Getting to grips with the problem

Like so much else, if action about office politics is taken to extremes the process becomes essentially destructive. At best, it creates an unhappy atmosphere in a department or indeed, in a whole organisation. At worst, its effects are tangible and show themselves in a hundred different ways around the organisation—lower productivity, higher staff turnover, less-satisfied customers, wasted time and lost opportunities.

If the organisation suffers, then so do the people, and even those who have put self interest exclusively first are not then immune.

66 We're all in this together. By ourselves. 99

Lily Tomlin

But it need not be like that. All the interactions and processes referred to in this book as so easily taking on a political overtone can,—handled differently—handled well, in a spirit of collaboration and with common purpose—create something extra. There is no unwritten law that says that meetings cannot reach decisions, that delegating—done wisely—cannot work out, or that communication, management and a host of other processes cannot be handled so that the organisation, as well as its people, prospers.

That is not to say that if you simply put the organisation first you will automatically survive and prosper. Would it were so easy. Of course, you have to stand up for yourself. The world will not seek out your good ideas or the contributions you can make nor will the organisation—at least not without some prompting. You have to seek out the opportunities yourself and if you are a manager, you must help your people do likewise. Give them the credit for the individual things that they make or contribute to make things go well. You can take the credit for finding, keeping and leading the team. In that way, things are really made to happen. It does not matter what the task is. It will be done more effectively in an atmosphere of trust and commitment—in which the common interest is in getting the job done for the good of all rather than just scoring points along the way. So whatever the activity—a meeting, a report to be written or a project to be managed—if you tackle it in the right spirit, you will get not only the job done but your efforts noticed as well. Overall, you have to manage yourself, the people you work with, the situations and environment you work in in a way that allows you to meet both your organisational—job—and personal goals.

❝You have a shilling. I have a shilling. We swap. You have my shilling and I have yours. We are no better off. But suppose you have an idea. We swap. Now you have two ideas. We have increased our stock of ideas by 100 per cent.**❞**

A.S. Gregg

In the real world, of course, you are unlikely to find yourself in an organisation where everyone operates solely for the common good of all—one where no one ever puts their own sectional and personal interests first. If you already have all the power and influence you want, a perfect secretary and the seat by the window, fine. If not, who can blame you if you keep at least half an eye open for anything that will help your cause.

There are no magic formulae to organisational success, at least not unless you can work one of the following 'Ten ultimate winning ploys'—success is a matter of awareness and application. If you are good at spotting the opportunities and taking advantage of them, you will get a step or two ahead. And if you go on doing so you will remain ahead of the game.

At least for the moment.

Check out the quiz that follows. It can provide an honest and comprehensive assessment of your chances (though at this stage, given the tone of the book you are not really expected to believe that).

Ten ultimate winning ploys

- *Marry the boss's son or daughter. (But consider whether this would be an improvement on not getting on in the organisation.)*

- *Marry the boss. (But consider as above and do not do so if you have already married the son or daughter. Not only is that taking the belt and braces concept too far—remember that the penalty for bigamy is two mother-in-laws.)*

- *Win the lottery. (And remember to actually buy a ticket. It does improve your chances and just dreaming about the possibility of serious drop dead money can make you feel better with your lot.)*

- *Take out a contract on the boss. (But be prepared to manage the company you may then control from prison—something that will bring a whole new meaning to the phrase 'insider trading'.)*

- *Buy the organisation. (But be prepared to spend the rest of your life fending off other predators and the bank from which you borrowed the money.)*

- *Get someone else to buy the company for you. (But, if it is an investor, remember that investors have a depressing habit of wanting their money back. You could always combine this with an earlier ploy and marry someone who will buy it for you as a wedding present.)*

- *Leave the organisation and start your own. (Then even if it remains small, you can console yourself with the thought that it is all yours—as I do.)*

- *Steal the organisation. (These days, that may be as easy as altering a few lines in some computer record—something that might make you feel a bit vulnerable if you already own it.)*

- *Arrange a coup, otherwise known in business circles as a 'management buy-out'. (This implies some allies, maybe you can find one such who has the necessary money, or the bank in his pocket.)*
- *Arrange a merger with another organisation. (Clearly, with the guarantee that you will have a prime position in the new combined organisation—preferably with a good and written contract to back it up.)*
- *Engineer a disaster of such magnitude that the organisation is made bankrupt. (And hover at a discreet distance, ready to pick up the pieces—they may be small pieces, but maybe one of them, a brand name perhaps, will give what will then be your new entity a good start.)*

<u>*Note*</u>: *Astute readers (and compulsive mathematicians) will have noticed that there are eleven 'Ten ultimate winning ploys'. Astute politicians will have realised this was intentional.*

<u>*Moral*</u>: *always have one more up your sleeve than is expected.*

There are of course other ploys, completely divorced from your immediate organisational life, that might give you a financial boost. Why only this morning, I had an e-mail from someone in Nigeria wanting assistance shifting some money around. It was a lot of money. Maybe I could …

> **❝**Just because you are paranoid it does not mean they are not out to get you.**❞**
>
> *Graffiti*

CHECKLIST: How high can you go?

The following checklist will enable you to see how well you will survive and prosper in the organisation.

It will be clear at this stage that there is no magic formula to organisational success. Those who survive and prosper need a variety of talents, a healthy dash of deviousness and some considerable tenacity and application. However, allowing that the details of what you do are important, there are some key factors that all aspiring office politicians will certainly need:

- Knowledge of what is going on around you (and this means good sources of information)
- Understanding of which people really have the influence in the organisation (rather than just who has the titles)
- Sufficiency of the right people, influencers or sources of information, who will assist you (whether voluntarily, unknowingly, or because you twist their arm)
- A high order of ability to communicate, verbally, in writing (formally and informally) and in every other way necessary
- The 'right' image (whatever you have judged this to be—high profile or virtually invisible)

- The patience of a saint (and if not, then at least the appearance of one)
- Sufficient assertiveness (but not so much that your very appearance causes others to batten down the hatches)
- Organisational and management ability (so as to manage your time, people, projects and yourself)
- To be quick on your feet (with an eye for the main chance or opportunity and the wit to take advantage of it)
- The ability to stand back and take the broad view (which often means a long term one too)
- A degree of ruthlessness (recognising both that competition is about eliminating the opposition and yet, that tyrants have few friends)

Rate yourself on the scale from 1 – 6 on each of these factors.

1 - Excellent (I can write a book on it)
2 - No problem
3 - Will be alright on the night
4 - Well maybe
5 - Finally, needs working on
6 - Do not even think it is necessary

If there are too many 5's and 6's resign yourself to a life of being trodden on, and consider buying the boss strawberry flavoured boot polish to, at least, make licking them a little more palatable. If, at the other end of the scale, you rate yourself consistently 2, then you are probably doing well; but remember some people will have their knives out for you and you need to be ever watchful. If you rate yourself 1 consistently, then you are certainly doing well, and *everyone* is likely to have their knives out for you.

Remember too that the higher you go, the longer the drop back becomes, and the harder the fall. As the man who fell off the skyscraper said as he passed the tenth floor, "Well, I'm alright so far." It only seemed that way. So, whether you are at the top of the scale or somewhere in the middle, keep working at it; and try not to worry—at least not unless you get paid for it. This may actually be possible. There is a story told of someone applying for the post of Director of Worrying. "What we want," said the interviewer, "is someone who can worry constructively day in, day out, for $20,000 a month." "You'd really pay me that much a month just to worry?" said the applicant. "Well," said the interviewer, "that's your first worry."

And while you are not worrying, keep your eyes open—especially the ones at the back of your head.

If your calculated rating depresses you, and everything that you have read here paints a picture of a maelstrom of political intrigue and uncertainty, and if you feel that being immersed in this kind of atmosphere full time may get you down, fear not. Help is at hand. If you feel things are getting on top of you, just register for a stress management course.

Such a course will, according to one course prospectus, "help you distinguish the positive and negative effects of stress; it will review personal coping behaviour and generally provide a very expensive way of being told to keep a sense of proportion and not to worry." As the old saying goes, "You die if you worry, and you die if you don't." Successful office politicians do not worry. They may be concerned, they may anticipate problems, they certainly plan ahead and take action to cover every eventuality—but they do not just worry. Or if they do then they may well contract terminal anxiety and die of a heart attack before they get to the top. So, resolve to be successful and stop worrying about everything, or give up the unequal struggle and book that course place now. There, you will learn about such things as ziargic tension, the upset you feel when you have to leave a task unfinished. Clearly, people who worry about that should never attempt to write a book—there are many days during the writing where you finish with more to do. Indeed some days, I find I finish in the middle of … a sentence.

Nevertheless, once you join such a group, you put your worries behind you and relax, then you may find yourself in the position of being distinctly one-up—the only unworried person in a class full of nervous wrecks. Which is rather like being the only person sufficiently well organised to arrive on time at a time management course. Once you have engineered yourself to the top of the class, then you can consider returning to the office and rejoining the fray.

One final piece of advice: watch what goes on around you and see the broad picture. Listen to everything and do so very carefully. Never close off your options until you must, but once the iron is really hot, strike. All these tactics will help you do a better job and do better in it.

And never settle for one of anything useful, including pieces of advice, if more than one is available.

> 66 I have a new philosophy. I am only going to dread one day at a time. 99
>
> *Charlie Brown (Peanuts)*

While the focus throughout this text has been largely internal, your progress relates too to the success of the organisation for which you work. If not all is well with that—see below—then you may need to take steps to relocate and think hard about getting the timing right. So do not get shut away, eyes down, and fail to see what the whole organisation is doing.

From the Megalomania Press Cuttings file:
- "Megalomania—another successful year"
- "Record bonuses for Megalomania management"
- "Megalomania's meglawidget market share up"
- "Is all well at Megalomania?"
- "Drop in Megalomania's sales"
- "Competitive pressure put on Megalomania"
- "Megalomania Shares crisis as competition intensifies"

- "Key players leave Megalomania - crisis deepens"
- "Megalomania taken over by rival"
- "Management at Megalomania must have taken eye off ball"
- "Many redundancies in wake of Megalomania take-over"
- "Megalomania name dropped as combined company consolidates"
- "Megalomania?"
- "What was that company...?"

Moral: Whatever the opposition are like within your organisation, they are for certain more dangerous outside.

Key guidelines to success

This story is worth noting.

There is a story from long ago of the courtier sentenced to life imprisonment by a medieval King for some small misdemeanour. After he had languished in his squalid cell for a while, he had an idea and sent a message to the King promising that, if he were released, he would work night and day and that, within a year, he would teach the King's favourite horse to talk.

This amused the King, and he ordered the courtier released and sent to work in the royal stables. The courtier's friends were pleased to see him released, but frightened for him too; after all they reasoned horses cannot talk, however much training they receive.

"What will you do?" they asked. "Many things can happen in a year," he replied. "I may die, the King may die; or, who knows—the horse may talk."

A final rule: *Always remain optimistic. You never know what may happen, and what does may change things in your favour.*

What is more, you may be able to change what happens. I like the courtier's story above and always feel that by the time the year was up, he would have come up with another cunning plan to keep him out of jail.

Read On...

Most books, if they intend to be the definitive work on their chosen topic (as this surely does), end with a list of further reading: a bibliography.

There is no reason for this volume to be any exception, but it does so with one difference. Most command you to actually read the books listed. Far be it for me to suggest otherwise (and some further suggestions follow), but for those aiming to be politically 'ept' in the office, there is another consideration—those books that will reflect best on you if others believe that you have read them. Indeed, like the producers of mustard, who make their profit not from the portion eaten, but from that left on the side of the plate, there are those who comment similarly about business book publishers. It is said that their profit comes, not from the books bought and read, but from those which sit untouched on the shelf. What an awful thought, enough to make any author worry (though, as I have said, I do not do that).

So, what can you, to advantage, put on your bookshelf? Whilst the following list does not presume to be comprehensive, those mentioned are worth considering and give you an idea of how to approach the process of selection.

Ten suggestions for your bookshelf

1. All those books listed behind the title page of this book (to demonstrate your inherent good taste and support for impoverished authors).

2. Some of the management classics, whose titles you will know like *In Search of Excellence*, with at least one or two being more than 10 years old (so that people will assume that you have been busy improving yourself for some time). Ditto classic authors, like Peter Drucker and Tom Peters.

3. Several in much thumbed paperback format (implying that you bought them yourself, and read them avidly on every train and plane you sit in, and long into the night).

4. Some on 'Fashion' elements of management, past and present, so that such terms as M.B.O., T.A., and Lateral Thinking are visible on the shelf.

5. Something humorous (to show that, though it may not always appear so, you do have a sense of humour).

6. Several that are about topics beyond your present area of responsibility (to show that you plan for the future and take an interest in the broad picture).

7. Some with current buzzwords in the title, but keep them up to date, people must either recognise them immediately or say to themselves—"What's that?"—not see them as old hat.

8. Several which imply considerable technicality or

numeracy—or both—(to worry those who are not so technical).

9. A few general titles, novels perhaps, with good business lessons in them. For instance James Cavell's book *Shogun*, which is an excellent read, and contains more about the art of strategy than most books specifically on the subject. (This means that when colleagues ask you why you have that in the office, you can explain as if you feel it is something everyone knows.)

10. At least one signed by the author (implying that you mix in circles different from, indeed better than, your peers). To start this process, send this book—together with a cheque for the purchase price—to the author, and it will be signed and returned at once. (The book that is, not the money.)

With all such books it adds significantly to the positive impression your possession of them gives if they have bookmarks, or yellow post-it notes, marking various pages in them. Do not just stick them in at random though, someone may ask what it is you have marked in them.

> 66 There are two motives for reading a book; one, that you can enjoy it; the other, that you can boast about it. 99
>
> *Bertrand Russell*

Last, one book not to have on show is this one. Or rather there could be advantage to you in having it around, but do not allow other people to read it. After all, you want to cultivate the impression that you know something that they do not, and the author wants them to buy their own copy—every little royalty payment helps. So, actually, maybe you should buy all the copies you see in local book shops just to prevent your corporate adversaries from getting their scheming hands on one.

Now, on a serious note, this book, though presented in a light hearted style, is intended to contain some serious— and potentially useful—messages. Therefore, in classic bibliography style, I would highlight just a few ideas of a manageable number of books that reading this might lead you to find of additional use. Topics relating directly to the content here include:

Career management: this is a necessity these days, not an option—my book *Detox Your Career* (Cyan) sets out essential approaches to what is necessary.

Communication: it is simply not possible to thrive in an organisation and ignore your communications skills. I have written on this in:
How to craft a successful presentation (Foulsham)
There's no need to shout! (Cyan)
Successful negotiation (How to Books)
How to write reports and proposals (Kogan Page)

You would expect me to mention my own writing, but I also recommend the following:

Brilliant Business Connections by Frances Kay (How to Books), which is in my view, an excellent and useful review of networking, a skill in which every office politician must excel.
Body Language by Alan Pease (Sheldon Press)

❝ A library is a thought in cold storage. **❞**
Herbert Samuel

Look to the Future

Like me, you may have sometimes dreamt. In one such dream I saw the future.

In the future organisations will work in an atmosphere of harmony and goodwill. In the future bosses will be supportive, trusting and likeable, and will not put you down or touch you up and suggest you attend an overseas conference with them (unless you want them too). They will make all their decisions with the implications for their staff foremost in their minds and not keep people in the dark, just because they can.

In the future you will have security and when you come back from holiday you will not find someone else in your office and a brown envelope with your name on it waiting for you.

In the future organisations will provide a fair remuneration for all their staff. They will approve all expense claims without haggling (even those that may be slightly suspect), not demand that you work ridiculous hours and put a decent coffee machine on every floor (and allow time for people to drink it and provide china rather than paper cups to drink it from).

In the future colleagues will be on your side, when they say you can trust them they will mean it and no one will ever come into your office and say, "Can you spare a minute?" And then waste 20 minutes or more.

In the future when people say, "You can tell me, I would never betray a confidence," they will be sincere (though a death penalty would help ensure this is so).

In the future voice mail will not exist, people will talk to each other and there will be time to do so. And they will listen too.

In the future your ideas will be listened to, appreciated and rewarded (and your boss will not tell everyone that they were his own).

In the future meetings will be short, useful and fun.

In the future there will be no infighting, no deception and no one will act deviously to get their own way.

In the future you will be able to rely on good luck, your career will flourish and you will be able to trust everyone and everything (except a dream).

However: for the moment you need to deal with reality. As a T-shirt I saw recently put it:

Yeah – I know. Get over it.

The corporate jungle looks set to remain just that. Nothing looks to be about to radically change its nature and a competitive, even sometimes hostile, environment will continue to prevail and be the lot of those who work in any organisation.

It is best for you to be prepared to take systematic, precise, purposeful and on-going action to survive and thrive in it. You must deal with all the inevitable elements of office politics involved and actively manage all those things that can lead to career success. And, perhaps, in addition, you should deploy just an occasional touch of judicious deviousness now and then. Go for it. I wish you well.

> **❝** Not a shred of evidence exists in favour of the idea that life is serious. **❞**
>
> *Brendan Gill*

About the Author

Patrick Forsyth has himself had a successful career; or certainly he likes to think so. He now runs his own company, Touchstone Training & Consultancy, specializing in the improvement of marketing, sales, and communications skills, and says he has now "found an employer I can really get on with."

He began his career in publishing and worked happily in sales, in promotion and marketing there, before escaping to something better paid just ahead of terminal poverty. He then worked for the Institute of Marketing (now the Chartered Institute), first in research, latterly in the promotion of their training products and publications. He helped set up an export assistance scheme and then moved into consultancy, first in a management marketing position. Much against his better judgment initially, he was soon persuaded to get involved in client work and began to undertake consulting assignments and conduct training courses.

His work also began to take on an international

dimension. He helped set up offices in Brussels and Singapore and began to work and lecture overseas. He still travels regularly, especially to South East Asia, and has, over the years, worked in most countries in continental Europe, including the former Eastern Bloc. Other, more occasional, destinations have included America, Australia, East Africa, Argentina, and Borneo.

After some years at director level in a medium-sized marketing consultancy, he set up his own organization in 1990. He conducts training for organizations in a wide range of industries, and has conducted public courses for such bodies as the Institute of Management, the City University Business School, and the London Chamber of Commerce and Industry.

In addition, he writes on matters of management and marketing in a variety of business journals, and is the author of more than 50 business books, corporate publications and training material.

Books in the Business Solutions Series

EFFECTIVE DECISION MAKING
10 steps to better decision making and problem solving | Jeremy Kourdi

BRILLIANT COMMUNICATION
5 steps to communicating your message clearly and effectively | Patrick Forsyth

THE NEW RULES OF ENTREPRENEURSHIP
What it really takes to become a savvy and successful entrepreneur | Rob Yeung

GREAT SELLING SKILLS
How to sell anything to anyone | Bob Etherington

THE NEW RULES OF JOBHUNTING
A modern guide to finding the job you want | Rob Yeung

MANAGE YOUR BOSS
How to create the ideal working relationship | Patrick Forsyth

GREAT NEGOTIATING SKILLS
The essential guide to getting what you want | Bob Etherington

SURVIVING OFFICE POLITICS
Coping and succeeding in the workplace jungle | Patrick Forsyth

ESSENTIAL TIME MANAGEMENT
How to become more productive and effective | Brett Hilder

SIMPLY A GREAT MANAGER
The fundamentals of being a successful manager | Mike Hoyle & Peter Newman